"With her revealing and introspective account of growing up in post-1989 China, Kan fills a void in contemporary literature on the country. While the profound societal shake-up that unfolded during that period has left everyone of her generation with a remarkable story, few have possessed such skill and courage in telling theirs."

—Eric Fish, author of *China's Millennials: The Want Generation*

under
red
skies

THREE GENERATIONS OF LIFE,

LOSS, AND HOPE IN CHINA

KAROLINE KAN

 hachette
BOOKS

NEW YORK   BOSTON

Hachette Books
Hachette Book Group
1290 Avenue of the Americas
New York, NY 10104
hachettebookgroup.com
twitter.com/hachettebooks

First Edition: March 2019

Hachette Books is a division of Hachette Book Group, Inc.
The Hachette Books name and logo are trademarks of Hachette Book Group, Inc.

The publisher is not responsible for websites (or their content) that are not owned by the publisher.

The Hachette Speakers Bureau provides a wide range of authors for speaking events. To find out more, go to www.hachettespeakersbureau.com or call (866) 376-6591.

Library of Congress Cataloging-in-Publication Data

Names: Kan, Karoline, 1989- author.
Title: Under red skies : three generations of life, loss, and hope in China / Karoline Kan.
Description: First edition. | New York : Hachette Books, 2019. | Includes index.
Identifiers: LCCN 2018036323| ISBN 9780316412049 (hardcover) | ISBN 9781549199837 (audio download) | ISBN 9780316412032 (ebook)
Subjects: LCSH: Kan, Karoline, 1989—Family. | China—Biography. | Women—China—Biography. | Intergenerational relations—China. | China—Social life and customs. | Social change—China. | China—Social conditions—1949-
Classification: LCC DS779.49.K36 A3 2019 | DDC 951.06/10922 [B] —dc23
LC record available at https://lccn.loc.gov/2018036323

Printed in the United States of America

LSC-H

10 9 8 7 6 5 4 3 2 1

To my family

Contents

PART II: THIRD GENERATION

Author's Note

My parents always used to say I was a "strange" child. In the 1990s and early 2000s, when I was growing up, my favorite thing to do after school was to follow the adults around like a little tail and listen to them tell stories. They called me *genpichong*, or "bum beetle," because I stuck to them like glue.

No matter whether they were talking to me or to each other—whether it was my grandmother, mother, aunt, or the neighbor's wife—I would always sit silently beside them, prick up my ears, and let my mind roam through the enchanting world of their stories. These women had little formal education, but the way they spoke was colorful and warm and delicately captured the moment. They talked in my grandmother's dim kitchen, under a willow tree in our yard, or in my neighbor's cabbage garden, their hands constantly occupied with never-ending chores like sewing patches, making soup, or clearing the table.

Some of the stories were mysterious, as though from a book of fairy tales. Weasels danced and imitated humans by singing in the village temple. River ghosts enticed villagers to jump to their deaths in the stream. Broom spirits held lanterns to light the way for people walking in the dead of night. The older women used spirits and ghosts to explain things they could not understand.

Then there were the real stories, which were just as fascinating.

My great-grandfather confessed to so-called "crimes" he had committed during the Cultural Revolution, such as reading and owning books written by Confucius or listening to the Peking opera, which during that time was disparaged as elitist and against the Communists' spirit of revolution, which sought to fight against the old way of feudalism and bourgeoisie.

My grandfather used his hat to hide the rice he'd stolen from the public kitchens to prevent his children from starving to death during the Great Famine.

My uncles had destroyed people's homes and tombs as Red Guards under Chairman Mao Zedong's regime. I heard stories of how a relative had fled to Taiwan after the civil war but could not return home for over half a century, and how political shifts had prevented my father from attending college, which became his life's biggest regret.

These were the first—and best—history lessons I ever had. And from these oral histories, I understand how my story is connected to China's.

In China's history, I've learned how ordinary lives can be upended by the political affairs of a nation. I learned how small changes could together alter the entire course of a country's future.

My dream became to write about the people I knew and loved and to tell their stories, as well as to write my own, free from government censorship and the Communist Party's narrative. I believe these stories deserve to be told, and I consider myself fortunate to have a platform to do so; many Chinese people never have a chance to make their voices heard.

For years, I buried my plan deeply in my chest. Almost all the memoirs I read in Chinese were about famous people. Nobody in my life had ever written a book—let alone a book in English. When I tried to sit my family members down for formal interviews, they would shrug me off. "There is nothing to say," they protested. "Everybody has this kind of story." They did not want to revisit the past; the right attitude was to focus on the future. They were afraid of saying the wrong thing or something that would get them in trouble, thanks partly to decades of censorship.

So instead of going to them as a journalist, I listened to them as a daughter, a granddaughter, a niece, and a friend. We lived together, and their stories appeared in day-to-day gossip and arguments, the routines of daily family living. I had to be patient, and let the stories flow to me on their own, while still asking questions until I came to understand the truth.

The stories piled up in my diary, notes without a clear purpose. Then, before I realized it, they became a part of me. Now, years later, I can still see, smell, hear, and feel the days and nights when I learned and lived these stories: the light fragrance of the flowers of the Chinese scholar tree on spring afternoons, the orange light in my grandparents' bedroom, the crying cicadas and frogs on summer nights. I wrote in my composition classes, at home, and at work.

I pitched personal essays to foreign newspapers and magazines like the *New York Times* and kept searching for the right home for the stories stored up inside me.

This book means more to me than just sharing stories about my family and myself, and what it means to be a Chinese millennial. Tens of millions of stories like ours make up the present-day complexity of what is China. Through these stories, I hope readers from all around the world can snatch a glimpse of how we came to be—of what our families went through to shape China into the country it is today.

As a Chinese millennial, I want to show the humanity behind the cold economic figures and classifiers associated with China, to reveal the emotions, choices, and compromises, the courage, love, and hope we share with people around the world. Like our counterparts everywhere, we defy single-word descriptions.

China has areas of rapid development but also miles of backwater. It is not only a global power but also a place where many still suffer from crippling poverty. Its technological advances make international headlines daily, but its rural schools still lack qualified teachers; and though we're pledged to the Communist Party, Chinese people live for the next Hollywood blockbuster, just like everybody else. To understand China and Chinese people, you have to imagine yourself there, to think what you might do in the circumstances experienced by families in this book, to have lived through certain politics and cultural traditions shown here. It is easier to blame China than to understand it; it is easier to judge Chinese people than to get to know them.

But I believe the rewards for striving to do so are great—as are the risks for failing to try.

When writing this book, I often asked myself: Why should people around the world be interested in my stories about life in China? Some of the reasons are obvious: China has the world's second-largest economy and is the number one trade partner for many countries. China plays a central role in international affairs.

The subtler reason is that the lives of young Chinese people increasingly overlap with their peers around the world. Young Chinese factory workers produce goods that are bought by consumers in America, Canada, and Europe. When the streets of Washington, DC, or Berlin or Vancouver fill for women's marches, university students in China are inspired by them. We stand together in rejecting what society tells us is "right" and "wrong."

The real China is not only comprised of the one shown in the daily news cycle.

In recent years, several books have been written about Chinese millennials, but mostly by foreign authors. I respect many of these, because they inspired me to write my own. Globally, the voices of young Chinese—especially those of young Chinese women—are often neglected.

I may have been born and raised in China, but I am constantly learning new things about it. This is my story and my family's story. It is a story of China, and it is my honor to share my country with you...wherever you are.

Historical Timeline

1945-1949   **The Chinese Civil War** occurs between Chiang Kai-shek's Nationalist Party (Kuomintang, or KMT) and Mao Zedong's Chinese Communist Party (CCP). The conflict begins with deployments and military clashes as each side tries to position itself to control North China and Northeast China (Manchuria).

1949   Chairman Mao declares the founding of the **People's Republic of China (PRC)**. The Communist Party has been in sole control of China's government and army ever since.

1958-1960   Shortly after the People's Republic of China is founded, Chairman Mao aims to rapidly surpass the prosperity of the UK and the US with **the Great Leap Forward.** The party sets unrealistic production goals, including for agriculture and industry, requires participation from all farmers, and establishes collective farming.

1959-1961   An estimated 20–43 million people die of starvation in **the Great Famine,** caused by drought, poor weather, and the policies of Chairman Mao, such as the elimination of the four pests—rats, flies, mosquitoes, and sparrows—upsetting the ecological balance.

1966   **The Cultural Revolution begins.** To reconsolidate his power within the party and push back against capitalist and bourgeois values, Chairman Mao calls on the country's youth, the "Red Guards," to purge the "impure" elements of Chinese society and revive the revolutionary spirit. The Red Guards attack, imprison, torture, and kill tens of millions of people, including party leaders, intellectuals, artists, and former landowners.

1976   **Chairman Mao** dies and the Cultural Revolution ends.

1978   **Start of the "Reform and Opening Up"**—Mao's successor, Deng Xiaoping, believes China needs economic reform and commerce with the West. Farmers are given land contracts and allowed to work on plots individually instead of collectively. The Marxist economy is largely replaced by a capitalist economy, and private businesses are allowed to operate for the first time since the Communist takeover.

1980 **The One-Child Policy** is created to manage soaring birth rates. Later, rural families may have two children if their first child is a girl. The policy remains until 2015.

1983 **The People's Commune collapses**, in large part, due to the rise of individual farming and private enterprise.

The Chinese government launches a "**Strike-Hard Campaign**." Party leaders believe Reform and Opening Up brought about chaos and wrong ideas and that the justice bureau was too soft on crime. In three years, over one million people are arrested and tried, often on flimsy or fabricated evidence. Minor crimes are punished severely. Today, many injustices are still being discovered and the rulings overturned.

1989 **The Tiananmen Massacre (a.k.a. June Fourth Incident)** occurs. Young college students protest in Beijing's Tiananmen Square for political reform. They want democracy and freedom of speech, among other rights. On June 4, the government sends the army with tanks to stop the protestors. It is estimated that up to two thousand people were killed.

1992 **The Falun Gong** practice begins and spreads throughout the country. The Chinese government labels it a cult and bans Falun Gong in 1999. Tens of thousands of followers are arrested or imprisoned without trial.

1997 **Hong Kong** is handed back to the Chinese government, ending more than 150 years of British colonization.

1999 US-led **NATO troops bomb the Chinese embassy** in Belgrade, killing three Chinese journalists during the Kosovo War.

2002 **SARS**, or severe acute respiratory syndrome, the epidemic outbreak that spread through China, kills hundreds of people.

2012 **Xi Jinping becomes general secretary** of the Communist Party and chairman of the Central Military Commission.

2013 The National People's Congress elects **Xi Jinping president**. He is still the commander in chief today.

PART I

First and Second Generations

CHAPTER ONE

The Second Born

Chaoyang, 1988

During the summer of 1988, the cicadas in the willow tree beside the main village road never stopped crying. On one particular day, my mother, Shumin, returned home early from work in the family's rice field. She lay in bed, deeply worried, knowing that her father-in-law would be angry that she had come home early, but that it would be nothing compared to how he would react when he discovered the secret she had kept from him for more than a month: she was pregnant with a second child. It was the only crime she had ever committed in her thirty-two years.

As she lay contemplating her next move, she could see from her window the banners painted in looming red characters on the white walls of her neighbor's home:

> Giving Birth to Fewer and Healthier
> Children Will Lead to a Happier Life

The ridiculous signs were tokens of China's One-Child Policy. But my mother was doubtful of the banner's promise: She had only one child, her family worked very hard, yet still they did not have money or happiness.

Mom and my baba, Chengtai, led a typical Chinese lifestyle. They lived with his parents and his three unmarried siblings. In the eighties, most young couples lived with their relatives. Their home was also typical: a three-room brick house, facing the south, and a small hut in the yard. At that time, burnt-red bricks were new, fashionable, and a sign of wealth. Previously, homes were built using handmade adobe—a mixture of mud and straw that dried into bricks in the sun—which was much cheaper, but not as strong. My grandmother, or Nainai, Baba's mother, had encircled the yard with bamboo poles to fence off her vegetable garden. Chickens and rabbits roamed under the two willow trees. Once a month, Nainai would sell the eggs and rabbits at the farmers' market.

That is how they lived. And everything about it was... ordinary.

My mother had not told anyone, except Baba, about the pregnancy. She couldn't; there was already too much tension at home with her in-laws. If Mom didn't wake early enough to work, Nainai would pull a long face and tell the neighbors she was lazy. "Young married women today are nothing like what we used to be," Nainai would complain.

Their village, Chaoyang, was a fairly new community in Ninghe County. It was rebuilt after the great Tangshan earthquake in 1976, which resulted in 240,000 deaths. After the earthquake, survivors built Chaoyang, which means "facing the sun," in hopes of a brighter future.

It is not known when people started to settle in Ninghe County—records were not kept. The old men, with their long, white goatees, said our ancestors had settled during the Qing dynasty (1644–1912) to escape a famine. I always loved listening to the old men talk about the village's history, their eyes closed and one hand stroking their beards. For hours, they'd squat in the shadows, chatting. They were the modern griots and storytellers.

My mom was raised in a different village but adapted easily to Chaoyang. Like her own hometown, it was small and everyone knew each other. Every woman in the village was from another place—this was the way of it—and it was the men whom we relied on for the best stories of our village.

In such a small place, rumors couldn't be tamed for more than a day, and this also worried my mom that morning. There were about five hundred people in Chaoyang, and on only three streets; one paved with asphalt and the other two with red bricks. Folks living in the houses along the asphalt road were considered fortunate. It was the smoother, more modern-looking street, and on rainy days, it didn't have little water pits like those that collected in the cobbled roads. The village chief had an asphalt road in front of his office, which spoke volumes about it as a symbol of status. Those with homes like ours, on the brick road, would build their houses taller and grander, as though to make up for an inferior feeling.

My family, the Kans, worked together on more than ten *mu*—over 1.6 acres—of farmland. In those days, the climate was wet enough to encourage the villagers to plant rice. Ninghe was famous for its rice, reeds, and fish. In the beginning of the twentieth century, when my grandparents were young, everyone in Ninghe depended on those resources to make a living. Before the first bridge in Ninghe was built, villagers would cross the river using wooden dinghies. A screen of tall reeds on the riverbank stretched like waves in a green sea. But when I was a child in the mid-1990s, Ninghe started to suffer from drought, and the fish died from water pollution. Soon, corn and cotton—which required less irrigation—replaced the lush rice.

It took a lot of work from the entire family to run the farm. They'd set out to work in the early morning, when the water in the paddy field was still cold. In their farmers' clothes—wide-legged pants and loose gray shirts—they were like uniformed ants.

Mom was a pretty woman by Chinese standards, with big, smoky eyes and a small nose. She would tie up her long mane in a scarf and let it hang to hide her neck from the sun. She was lighter skinned than most women in the village, and had a few freckles. Women with freckles were said to have a wild spirit. She was also a strong farmer. Mom would walk barefoot in the field for hours, row by row. She was small but sturdy, focused, and fast. While other women rested at the field ridge to drink water, Mom would continue treading the fields.

But to the dismay of her in-laws, she worked in the field on the weekends only. During the week, she went to a job she loved, a place where she could wear her floral printed shirts and dresses made from soft polyester fabric.

She was a teacher at the primary school in her parents' village, Caiyuan. She did this even in early summer—a crucial farming time—and so she was labeled as stubborn.

The family had to work fast and hard if they wished to bring in a good harvest, and it was difficult to satisfy my paternal grandfather, Wengui. At the time, farmers did not have access to many machines, and there were only a few horses, so labor was mostly by hand.

In 1982, China embarked on significant land reform. Whereas in the past a village would have worked the land together—communally—this new system rented land to individual family units. So, the more time a farmer spent on his land, the better the harvest would likely be in the autumn and the more income his family might accumulate. This notion made Grandfather Wengui the family's drill sergeant—he needed everyone to be swift and available—and he had a *big* problem with my mom's choice to divert her time elsewhere.

★   ★   ★

The land reform led to the collapse of the People's Commune, an agricultural cooperative initiated in 1960 during the Great Leap Forward, a campaign led by Chairman Mao that set unattainable production goals with the sheer objective of overtaking Western countries within a few years. The government decreed that the production of steel in 1959 should be four times the volume of 1957, and the production of grain should double within two years. Their mission was clear.

Mom was a little girl then, and told me that one day the village chief had gone to her house and announced that, henceforth, they would be able to eat beef and potatoes every day. Everyone was amazed; it was the best food the villagers could imagine having access to. They didn't care that they'd have to share it. Her mother made the best meat dishes. She and her brothers were ecstatic, but one day she came home to find her mother quietly weeping. Local officials had arrived to take away the family's dining table and their only iron wok—a prized possession in most Chinese households. "You don't need these anymore," the village chief had said sternly. "Everyone will eat together in the public canteen." He removed a notebook from the chest pocket of his blue Mao uniform—a dark two-piece suit with baggy pants and a four-pocket collarless blazer. He made note of the items he had confiscated. "It's time to say good-bye to the old way of living, in which you care only for yourself and your own family. In the People's Commune, we will support each other."

But the meals at the canteen were short lived. The first month, there was beef and potatoes, the second month only rice and boiled vegetables. In the last month, the cooks didn't have enough grain to supply three meals a day. Within three years, although the villagers had continued to work communally on the farmland, the canteens were closed. The government later announced that the public canteens were a "great proletarian revolutionary experiment" and the villagers were allowed to return to their own kitchens. They had been reduced to rats in a lab.

Though productivity was low, village officials around

China would report grain production several times more than what they obtained in order to impress the higher-ups. When the exaggerated figures were registered, the central government had collected a disproportionate amount of grain, leaving tiny amounts for the localities. This contributed to the Great Famine, which lasted from 1959 to 1961, when tens of millions of people died from starvation. My mom vividly remembers walking with her father to the graves of our family's ancestors, where bitter wild grass tended to grow and which they would pick for dinner. She was four years old, and it was all they had to eat.

The Communists hoped the land reform of the 1980s, which allowed farmers to work on land owned by their families, would rekindle people's belief in socialism. However, villagers like Grandfather Wengui were doubtful. If there was anything he had learned from the war with Japan, the civil war, and the Cultural Revolution, it was to grab whatever fortune you could scrounge during peacetime, before chaos returned and things like food started to disappear again. Like the other villagers, Grandfather Wengui stopped complaining and started to invest all his time into the land he had.

★ ★ ★

Mom knew my grandparents would try to force her to have an abortion. They needed her to work, and a second child was illegal. If she had the baby, she would face a hefty government fine. But she wanted another child, and she vowed to Buddha that she'd walk to the Dule Temple one hundred miles away to thank him if he helped her. She and my father hoped they would be able to borrow money for the fine, and that she'd keep working throughout the pregnancy to save up.

Wengui didn't understand why Mom cared so much about teaching other people's children and not staying at home with her own. "How could you be so selfish? You leave your son for the whole day. What kind of mother are you?" Wengui said one afternoon when he and Mom were sitting on the floor of their front room, weaving a reed mat.

"I don't make much, but it helps that I can feed myself," she answered without raising her eyes from the mat.

Wengui roughly threw aside the hammer he had been using to tamp down the mat edge. "Feed yourself? The Kan family will feed you as long as you are still our daughter-in-law. Why do you need to go around like a woman who *pāotóulòumiàn*?" Wengui stressed *pāotóulòumiàn*, which means "go out to be seen in public" and is usually used to refer to women in a negative light.

Women were traditionally required to stay home and avoid contact with men other than close family members. *Pāotóulòumiàn* was common after Mao's revolution, when women were widely encouraged to work outside the home. But still, the traditional concept remained.

Wengui believed in those old values, that a wife was the property of her husband and his family. And Baba was not helpful. He was an obedient first son. A thin, hairy man, Baba had eyes that always looked at the ground when he spoke to his father—a sign of respect and meek, filial piety. He was afraid of Grandfather Wengui, but also cared too much about what people thought of him. Speaking up for his wife—or showing affection toward his wife or child—

could damage a man's reputation, and he did not want to be a laughingstock.

Baba had a very good memory and did well in school. He had been accepted by a prestigious medical university to major in surgical science in 1977, but Wengui refused to let his son go, saying he could do better than being a doctor, who was no better than a patient's servant in Wengui's eyes. So he turned down the offer and took the exam again the following year. But even though he passed a second time, the local education bureau disqualified him from applying to university, scolding him for "wasting the education resources the previous year." In desperation and pain, Baba returned to the farm and followed in his father's footsteps.

But in private, Baba listened to my mother more than his family knew. It was Mom's idea for him to buy a tractor so that he could haul bricks from a factory in a neighboring province at a lower price, then sell them to nearby villages. It brought in additional income for the family.

Born in the village, Baba had automatically received a rural *hukou*, not an urban one. *Hukou* was a household registration system that dictated where a person could go to school, get married, and work. Baba's *hukou* prevented him from getting a job in the steel or textile factories in the nearby town. He never did make it to college, but after his high school graduation, the family became financially dependent on him.

On the last day of each month, Baba would dutifully hand the money he earned to his mother. She would give pocket money to each family member before locking the rest in a black wooden cabinet.

As the fourth child, and the first girl, Mom was prohibited

from going to high school to help her family. But she continued to teach herself, and was very proud of her position as a full-time substitute teacher. Substitute teachers were not registered with the government, but were directly hired by the local schools. They had no insurance or contract. In 1977, 56 percent of China's school system was made up of substitute teachers due to the country's lack of qualified educators. Teachers were paid very little, hardly enough to survive on. Only a small group of teachers were promoted to permanent staff because the government's limited budget could not support so many registered teachers all at once. But Mom was eager for a promotion, especially with a new baby coming. At the same time, she could be fired for disobeying the One-Child Policy.

Surprisingly, and even though Mom knew all this, her pregnancy was not an accident.

Five years prior, just a few months after China implemented the One-Child Policy, my parents had my brother, Yunxiang. As the first son of the family, he was expected to continue the bloodline. The news of a grandson lit up Wengui's wrinkled eyes. Yunxiang had the Kan family's round face and steely black hair. I heard that on the day Yunxiang was born, the day of the Dragon Boat Festival, Grandpa lit a long ring of fireworks in celebration. Wengui was so pleased that he took my father to our ancestors' graves, where father and son knelt to give thanks for the blessing of a baby boy. Mom was not allowed to join them; women supposedly brought bad luck if they attended such ceremonies.

Though she loved her son dearly, she wanted a girl for

herself, and knew she'd have one. It would be her and Buddha's decision—not China's.

*   *   *

The sudden One-Child Policy of the 1980s bothered the unlucky old men in the village without grandsons. For some time, there had been discussion about how to control China's fast-growing population, which exploded after 1962, after the Great Famine. After eight years of war against Japan and another four years of civil war, in which tens of millions of people died, Chairman Mao called on people to have more children—dubbing women with many children "Heroine Mothers." In response to Chairman Mao's encouragement, my grandparents on both sides had seven children apiece.

Then, in 1983, China's census showed its population had grown to more than one billion, a two-thirds increase from the census in 1953. In hopes of curbing the population boom, China enacted the standardized, national One-Child Policy. It was the first time Chinese people had ever heard that birth should be controlled.

The policy began to take hold widely and quickly, with officials in all levels of government in charge of family planning. Chaoyang had the infamous Sister Lin, a short, strong woman in her early forties. She had three children but proudly defended the new policy. Mom said Lin had a cheerful appearance, but behind her back people called her a "smiley tigress" who "hid knives in her teeth." Every week, Sister Lin went door to door with brochures about the One-Child Policy. She was in charge of official paper-work for newborns, and though she never enforced abor-tions, everyone believed she was the person who reported married women's illegal pregnancies to the county's Birth Control Office. Otherwise, how would they have had the in-formation so quickly?

Sister Lin was unapologetic, and even the most well liked and admired, like Teacher Huang, were reported. Huang, a polite and gentle man who always wore neat blue trousers and a pen tucked into the breast pocket of his white shirt, was fired from the central middle school for having a second child. Despite being such a beloved teacher whose students regularly excelled academically.

There was also Farmer Lian, a short man with tanned skin who lived in the neighboring village and sometimes came to Chaoyang to sell his home-grown cabbage and radish.

"Lian will not be showing up this week; he has his own awful mess to deal with," Sister Lin said sternly to the group of women shopping for vegetables at the small morning market. "He delayed paying the fine for his second child again and again, and refused to open the gate when officials came by. They took a piece of wood from his yard and broke down the door. He had to hand over his tractor." Upon hearing such news, the vil-lagers would grow more afraid, which seemed to excite Sister Lin. She'd raise her chin higher. "You know, it's not robbery. It's called 'confiscation.'" A word they did not know.

A month after Yunxiang was born, Sister Lin knocked on

Mom's door. "Congratulations!" she said before stepping inside. "A boy!"

Mom struggled to sit up in bed to greet her. It is customary for women to stay in bed the first month after giving birth to both recover and receive guests. But it was clear that Sister Lin had come for more reasons than a congratulatory visit.

"When you think you've had enough rest, come see me. I'll write a letter to the hospital to get the birth-control ring put in," said Sister Lin. She stretched her neck closer to my sleeping brother. "It's wonderful that you have a boy," she whispered, "not like Xiu Feng's wife. She just had another girl. I am almost sure she'll sneak off and try for another one."

Mom nodded and promised not to have another child.

Six months later, Mom received a letter from the village committee instructing her to go to the local hospital to have an intrautcrinc ring put in her body. It was a new order from the Ninghe County Birth Control Office.

Every few months, the Birth Control Office would ask mothers with one child to come in for a B-scan ultrasound or an X-ray to ensure their intrautcrinc rings were still in the right place. Some women ran off to relatives' homes in other villages to hide and avoid the ring, the check, or the abortion, but this was only a temporary solution.

There was no escape.

Mom had heard that in a neighboring village, to punish two women who refused the ring, the Birth Control Office performed forced surgical sterilization. Mom was afraid but had also heard that the ring could be easily removed. That was safer than running.

She knew of women who tried to run but got caught, and she witnessed government officials forcing them into cars, sometimes even trucks with wooden benches in the back—used otherwise to take pigs to the slaughterhouses.

The women didn't know much about the intrauterine ring. They only knew from Sister Lin that once it was inserted into the uterus, it would prevent pregnancy. Sister Lin explained, using the diagrams set out in the government leaflets.

She also explained the difference between the ultrasound and X-ray. "You have to take off your clothes and bare your belly with the B-scan," she'd warn. "The X-ray is quicker and best, unless you want a male doctor touching you all over with a machine."

Many of the women were still too conservative to let a male doctor touch them and didn't like the idea of a miscellaneous object in their bodies, so, again, panic and rumors ensued.

"I heard they smear a kind of poison on the ring; that's how it stops women from getting pregnant," one woman reported at the market.

"My cousin said she bled for months after that goddamned thing was put in her body!" said another woman.

Five years after my brother was born there was still no sign of the law being overturned, as the old folks had predicted. Furthermore, the penalty for breaking it grew more severe. There were stories about unborn babies aborted at late-stage pregnancies. In my aunt's village, a woman was reported to the authorities when she was seven months pregnant. To ward off the officials, her family put diapers on the clothesline, where they could be easily seen. They said she'd had a premature delivery. When the birth-control officials came around to ask for the second-child fine, the pregnant woman sat in bed with quilts covering her body, and held a baby borrowed from relatives on her lap. The baby was clearly bigger than a newborn and the officers caught on. The woman and her family begged, cried, and pleaded with the officers, but they still took her in for a forced abortion.

To my mom's relief, her age gave her some respite: the Birth Control Office no longer scrutinized older mothers. She had to do a B-scan photo only a few times a year.

In the meantime, she had secretly consulted a doctor in her parents' village, and had the ring removed.

Three months later, at her next physical, she asked to have an X-ray rather than a B-scan. So many women were checked daily that the grumpy doctor would often rush them along, so my mom got by with a little trick. She put an iron ring into the pocket of her long coat and adjusted the pocket to the exact position where the intrauterine ring should show. When the photo was taken, all the doctor could see was that there was a ring in the right place.

But pregnancy was only the beginning of her troubles: How could she hide her growing stomach? How long could she keep her job? How would she consult a doctor if something happened to her? Where would she give birth? No hospital would accept her without a birth permit. And when the baby was born, where could she get enough yuan to pay the fine? These questions haunted her day and night.

She went to her mother for advice.

Her parents' village, Caiyuan, had a longer history than my dad's. The school where Mom worked had been a temple. It was destroyed in 1966 by Red Guards—a student organization during the Cultural Revolution (1966–1976)—who were encouraged by Chairman Mao to eliminate all remnants of the old China: "Old thoughts, old culture, old customs, and old habits," they pledged to remove.

Mom sat by the window in her childhood home, listening to her mother. "You never know what the government's policy will be tomorrow," said my grandmother Guiqin, "but if you have a second baby, the child will be there always. I say, have another. A boy would be good; a girl would be better. A daughter is her mother's closest companion."

When my mother told me about Guiqin's undying support to have me, I was both surprised and not. These were the willful women of my family. The women I come from. These women have pushed me to move forward and be unafraid and confident about my decisions, as they had to be in order for me to exist. They were born in a more difficult time than I was. Society, the government, and their families paid no heed to these women's ambitions and desires, but they fought against the merciless odds to make something out of very little.

Mom—afraid she would never be able to teach again—was not sure this was a notion my grandmother could relate to. Grandma Guiqin had no education, and had never worked outside the family home. She also never had the government stopping her from having the children she wanted. But Mom found relief in her mother's kind words. Though she wanted more for me, her daughter, than what my grandmother expected of her—she wanted me to be more than just her caretaker.

The June breeze sent Mom's thoughts blowing through the small window, into the waterlilies in the river running alongside their home. She remembered her childhood, when she would race in the wind with her brothers in the yard. She had always cherished the happiness of growing up with siblings and wanted Yunxiang to have such memories too.

"For women, family is more important than anything," my grandmother added, pulling Mom back from her thoughts. Mom nodded; there was no point in arguing with a woman born in 1924. Grandma Guiqin, pale and physically fragile, had married into my grandfather's village at the age of fifteen, and had never traveled farther than eight miles from her front door. "Try to hide the stomach for a few more months," Grandma advised as she pulled a blanket over herself. Even in June she couldn't bear the most gentle chill. "When it's big enough, who would kill a baby about to be born?" She grabbed Mom's hands and gently caressed them. "The older I grow, the more confused I get about life. Too many people ignore the law of the *lǎotiānyé*, the Heavenly Lord, and do bad things so proudly."

Mom nodded again.

"You know"—Grandma perked up—"Xiangju's husband works in the government. Why don't you ask her for help?"

Xiangju was Mom's best friend since childhood, and had always been a lucky girl. Her father, a teacher, was one of the few men who had appointed his daughter instead of his son to "inherit" his job. She had also married a local government worker.

There were many differences between my mom and Xiangju, but for reasons nobody understood, they were best friends. Xiangju was tough in nature—straightforward and competitive. Mom had thought of asking her for help but was too proud, in part because Xiangju hadn't forgiven her for marrying my father.

"What's so good about him, Shumin? He's a farmer," scolded Xiangju once in a fight. "He's nothing!"

No, Xiangju would be the last person she'd ask for help.

★   ★   ★

The first few months, Mom hid the pregnancy well. And in the cool autumn months, a long, loose coat always helped. On the night of the Mid-Autumn Festival, she stood facing the moon, put her palms together in devotion, and begged the goddess of the moon to bless her. Her belly remained small in the first few months, so she was hopeful. "Grow slower, baby," she whispered to me.

The first crisis came when Sister Lin showed up one day to tell her that there was a new physical check required of married women. This really worried Mom; a little coat trick wouldn't do now. Even the blurriest photo would reveal the baby in her womb. "So sorry, Sister Lin," she said. "I have to teach, you know. It's so close to the final exams and I really can't leave the students. I'll go to the hospital myself when the semester's over."

Sister Lin didn't insist: Other villagers had told her

Shumin was the last one she needed to worry about. "She's so eager to have a teaching job," they gossiped. "Of course she wouldn't have a second child."

Mom pushed back the checkup several times until even Sister Lin forgot about it.

She felt lucky. Her sister worked in a factory and told her that female workers had to report their period each month to show they were not pregnant.

Mom was one of only three teachers at her school, and though they didn't notice her belly in the first few months, by the winter her secret could no longer be contained—not from her colleagues or her in-laws.

She and Dad told their family about her pregnancy over dinner. "Shumin is pregnant," my dad said to his father.

Wengui pushed aside his bowl and sat silent. When the old man did that, nobody else at the table dared even move their chopsticks. It was the longest few minutes ever. Mom sneaked a glance at my dad, whose head was down in anticipation of his father's wrath.

Finally, Wengui said softly, "How are you going to deal with it? We don't have any money."

Then he picked up his chopsticks and began eating again, and everyone at the table followed. For the rest of the dinner, the only sound was chopsticks hitting rice bowls.

At this point, Mom had to follow her mother's advice. When she knew Xiangju would be visiting my grandmother, Mom made sure to be waiting at the house. She had no choice but to throw aside her pride and ask for help.

When Xiangju arrived, she entered carrying a basket of apples and bananas. She had newly permed hair, which made her look more elegant, Mom told her. Xiangju smiled and sat down. She picked up a handful of bananas. "This is what my husband brought home from town last week. We don't see it much in the village—southern fruits are not worth the money. They rot so fast."

She handed a banana each to Mom and Grandma Guiqin before she noticed Mom's bulging belly.

"Shumin? Are you pregnant again?"

"Yes," Mom confessed and proceeded to tell Xiangju about her situation. To her great relief, her friend was willing to help.

"I understand. My husband has been in charge of the birth-planning work since last autumn," she admitted. "I'm not very proud of what he's doing. But what can he do? Every village must control the numbers. They have to keep it under a certain number each year. If there's one more illegal baby born, the official's salary will be decreased." She took a deep breath. "What a goddamned job he has!"

They sat in silence for a while until suddenly Xiangju got up and quickly walked to the door and closed it, so the neighbors, who lived in the same yard, would not hear. She then sat close to Mom and whispered, "I have an idea. I'll let you know when the birth-control team is coming to inspect your village. I'll tell my husband that you haven't recovered from high blood pressure since you gave birth to Yunxiang, and that you can't bear the harassment right now. Trust me, nobody in the government wants to see an illegal baby, but nobody wants to see a dead woman either."

★   ★   ★

That chilly November in northern China, when the trees shed their leaves, people climbed on ladders to pick orange persimmons hanging ripe in their front yards. They bought and harvested cabbage, which they piled high into backyard storage and covered with hay, to prepare for the long winter.

The sky was so gray it seemed the first snow was already on its way. Mom had cleaned out her desk and announced that she wouldn't be returning. She no longer felt safe at the school; being in the same place all the time would only make it easier for the government to notice her and take her away for an abortion.

"I'm not sure if you'll want to return after the second one is born, but you can always come back," said the headmistress, Lao Li. She sipped tea from a white-enameled cup. "The children will miss you."

Mom held back her tears and said goodbye. She had never betrayed the government or the people around her so severely. For a moment, she strongly doubted the decision she had made, but then walked out of the school gate to sit on the back seat of Baba's bicycle for the ride home.

As my mother sat behind my dad, her heart pounded when she thought of the incident at home the previous weekend. As promised, Xiangju had informed her in advance of the birth-control team's visit to Chaoyang. Baba was not home. Mom decided to hide in the field and Yunxiang insisted on being with her.

The abandoned corn straw was high enough to hide her, and she held Yunxiang close, gently whispering to him, "Don't make a noise if you want to stay with Mommy. We have to hide from those people."

He understood, and squatted to hide his little body as well. He looked up at her and asked, "We are protecting little brother?"

She nodded, though they didn't know if the child in her belly would be a boy or a girl. She dared not visit a hospital. She'd had a dream that week in which a colorful snake was dancing in front of her, and the snake wore a flowered crown on its head. It was the year of the snake in the Chinese zodiac, and she believed the flowered crown indicated that she would give birth to a girl.

When she and Yunxiang came back, Baba had returned from work, brick dust thickly layered on his quilted cotton jacket.

"Father and Mother told the inspectors you were helping your sick aunt in another village," he said, "but I think they'll come again. Soon."

They ate dinner that night again in silence.

"I've heard that once you reach the eighth month, they won't do anything," Baba said, trying to console her quietly that night in bed. "Let's just make it through one more month."

★   ★   ★

In March 1989, I was born at home. It was midnight. Baba rode his bike to the neighboring village to knock on a local midwife's door for help. The midwife had been put on notice, so she was well prepared. When they arrived, everybody was waiting in our kitchen, which doubled as the living room. The midwife asked Nainai, Baba's mom, to help her, and told Wengui and Baba to wait outside. She said the birthing blood would bring bad luck to the men. Yunxiang was so excited he couldn't sleep. He walked here and there, and asked Grandpa and Dad again and again when he would meet his little brother. At 3:15 a.m., a loud crying sound came from the bedroom. Nainai came out with sweat on her forehead. "It's a girl," she cried. Mom told me later that she felt a wave of relief once she saw me. I had arrived, so they could no longer kill me. It would be a long road ahead, but she was happy that I had survived. My maternal grandfather, Laoye, named me Chaoqun, which means "to stand out from the crowd." It was a good name—for survival and difference would be the running themes in my life. Later, as a writer, I would adopt the pseudonym Karoline.

Not long after, my parents were ordered to pay the fine of 6,000 yuan for having me, which would ensure that I received a *hukou*—the ID that would enable me to enroll in school, marry, and receive healthcare. In 1989, the average annual income for people in Chinese cities was only a bit more than 1,000 yuan, the equivalent to $157, and in rural areas even less. So the fine equaled several years of my parents' and grandparents' incomes.

"I can't understand why you wanted to have a girl," my grandfather complained to my dad while hitting his pipe against the wall, cleaning out the ash perhaps more fervently than usual. He then stood in the open doorway, frowning and looking out at the paddy fields. The rice would soon be tall enough to thin the sprouts. Unfortunately, with his daughter-in-law tending to her newborn baby, he'd have even fewer hands to help.

"Days will be wasted," he muttered.

"We'll manage," said Baba.

Wengui lit the tobacco leaves in his pipe while looking out over his farm.

But, that spring, five days before my parents were due to pay the fine, he handed Baba a blue handkerchief. In it was 2,000 yuan. His life savings.

CHAPTER TWO

A Daughter's Promise

I have two birthdays. One is a secret and what I celebrate at home, and the other is written on all my official documents. Like my birth, this, too, was not an accident.

On the penalty notice that Sister Lin left my parents, she had underlined the words *Pay within two months*. But by the time the deadline arrived, my parents still needed 1,000 yuan in addition to what Wengui had given them and what they had saved. They were worried. The local Birth Control Office threatened that if they didn't register my birth in time, I would never be registered. And failing to obtain a *hukou* would condemn me to life as a "black child," a term used for those whose existence is not recognized by the government. According to the latest national demographic census done in 2010, China had about 13 million "black children" because their parents couldn't pay the fine. Without a *hukou*, they are unable to attend school, marry or work legally, or even get on a train.

Every week, the Birth Control Office chased my parents for payment. Sometimes, Sister Lin came; other times, the officials knocked on our door themselves.

"If you delay payment, the government will charge you more," shouted Sister Lin one day, peering over the fence to our backyard, where my mother was hanging laundry to dry.

Lin had just returned from the county's All Women Federation meeting, during which the director continued to pressure her to do more to collect the fines. The little tiger lady took her work seriously.

My mother put aside her clothes basket and unbolted the gate. "You can come in, Sister Lin, but the money won't grow from the dirt, will it? We are trying."

"Of course, but you have broken the law!" Lin sat on the stool. "The money is not for me! The fine you pay will go straight to the national treasury. Your second child is draining resources from our country, so this is your responsibility."

Mom doubted this was true. It was no secret that the Birth Control Office was a financially well-off branch of government—in our county, at least. Its officials had the best homes. The villagers believed that local bureaucrats—not national ones—decided the size of the fines for their own personal gain. There was a thick barricade between the *lǎobǎixìng*, or common citizen, and the government. At that time, there was no voting system in the county that enabled the villagers to choose officials directly. The *lǎobǎixìng* did not have access to the decision-making process in the citadels of the powerful. Mom knew this, so it made her angry that Sister Lin was suggesting the fee was an even trade.

It wasn't until June that my parents had gathered enough money...then there was the late fee.

I wasn't born in a hospital, so there was no documentation showing my exact birthday. How would the officials know if the payment was late? The only official who might know the exact day was Sister Lin. If she agreed to write a letter to the Birth Control Office stating my parents paid the fine on time, they would not come to the village to verify it.

This time Mom went knocking on Lin's door. She carried a bamboo basket, which contained a chicken my father had just killed, a pack of Zhōngnánhǎi—the most expensive cigarettes she could find—and three bottles of pickled peaches. My parents understood the power and necessity of such bribes. It was regarded as "gift giving," allowing people to develop relationships and, if needed, speed up bureaucratic processes.

My mother smiled as she placed the basket on Sister Lin's dinner table. "My husband and I wondered if it would be okay if we just say Chaoqun was born in April?"

Sister Lin peeked into the basket and then pushed it back toward my mother. "Aiya, what are you doing?" After a few rounds of pushing the basket back and forth, Lin put it in a closet. Sister Lin loved gifts, but it was an unspoken rule in China, even among close friends and relatives, to not accept gifts eagerly. You wouldn't want to give the impression that you were greedy. Whether sincere or faking it, a person would act it out, and sometimes acted so well that it looked like a real fight. "This is only my job. I won't accept the gifts but tomorrow I will go to the county government's office and tell your situation to my boss. He's a big smoker. I will try my best."

Soon enough, my parents received a letter from the Birth Control Office. That same day, Baba bicycled to the police station to register me. When he was handed the *hukou* notebook, it read "Birthday: April 21, 1989"—over a month later than my real birthday. He felt guilty for a moment but put the *hukou* notebook in his bag and quickly left the police station. He knew he couldn't give me a lot, but at least he could give me an identity. For this, he felt proud.

★   ★   ★

A few months later, Sister Lin came around again with another announcement from the Birth Control Office. They wanted all women who had two children to do a sterilization operation—tubal ligation. My grandparents, who were of Mao's era, understood that any government dictates should be perceived as the most "glorious, right, and great decision," and had learned to accept such demands without question. They ordered Mom to comply, but she was against the idea. Though she didn't plan to have more children, she couldn't accept losing one of the most important functions of her body. It was her body after all, and she believed it should be her choice.

Though they were just following the rules, the women who did undergo sterilization were mocked, and were becoming known as "the third gender." Many suffered from infections, their recovery often long and painful. When people ask me today why I advocate for a strong feminist movement in China, I think of the third gender. Those women did not have a voice, a way of putting a stop to what was happening to them. Today, more of us do.

Sister Lin kept a notebook in which she jotted down names of women who had been sterilized voluntarily. Months passed, the names in the book didn't increase, and the officials were champing at the bit to get more women to agree to the operation.

One day, when my mother was shopping, she was startled by a strident male voice coming through the speakers on every street corner. "Attention! Just received an order from the government: Women who already have two children must register with Sister Lin and get your tubal ligation operation done now! *All* mothers with two children. No exceptions..." The broadcaster also stressed that refusal to go to the hospital would mean that officials would take you there forcefully.

But Mom was ready to play cat and mouse again. She asked the doctor who had helped her give birth to Yunxiang for a letter with the hospital's stamp saying that she had almost died from serious anemia and hypertension during labor, which was true. When she knew the officials were coming to Chaoyang, she would go out to work with my father in other villages to sell bricks; however, the officials caught her twice and took her to the county clinic. Both times, she had been able to sneak away, in the shadows of the chaos.

But when they caught her a third time—two males and one female official—they had come specifically for her.

That day, my dad was not at home, and my grandparents were at a neighbor's playing mahjong, a popular table game that uses tiles instead of cards. My mother stood at the gate, refusing to get into the car. I was holding her legs, crying. Yunxiang rushed to the neighbor's house and called for my grandparents.

"She's a stubborn woman!" one officer yelled, pacing and smoking. He threw his cigarette butt to the ground. "Don't cry to us; this is just our job! I'm not going to lose my job because of you. Get in the car! Now!"

By the time my grandparents ran over, the officials had already pushed Mom into the back seat.

"Bring my coat, Yunxiang," she screamed.

The doctor's note was in there, along with a legal-sounding letter her brother—a lawyer—had written for her, in case of just this kind of emergency. She refused to give up. It was her body and she would protect it. She didn't know if the letter would help, but she'd try.

"My daughter," she wailed, reaching for me. "I'm taking her with me."

"She's too young!" yelled the officer.

But Mom pulled me in the car and held on for dear life. Neighbors, standing on their tiptoes with stretched necks, watched as it sped off, my mother restrained in the back seat, dragged away like a wild animal.

When the car arrived at the county's central clinic, a large crowd of women like my mom were waiting outside. The clinic didn't have enough rooms, so they had set up twenty or so tents for the operations. The smell of blood and sweat brewed in the air and, together with the cries and screaming, made my mom feel as if she were going to throw up. She looked around, left and right, trying to find an exit route, but the nurses were watching her closely. I was squirming desperately on her lap, my eyes closed and my hands over my ears. I didn't know what was going on, but I sensed that she was going to get hurt—either she or I—and so I held on to her as tightly as possible. She clutched the letter, her sweat soaking through the paper. I tugged on her sleeve, recalling what she had taught me to do when we were in the market: "If we're in a crowd, pull Mommy's sleeve and you won't lose your way." So I pulled and pulled.

A doctor who seemed to be in charge drew his finger down a list of names. Then, three, two, one, it was her turn.

It was so stuffy inside, the doctor removed his white lab coat and draped it over the back of a chair in the corner. He had been working without a break since early morning. His hair was unkempt, and his wrinkled shirt had come partially untucked. Through his large glasses, his eyes were bloodshot, with dark circles underneath.

"It says here that you've twice run away from the clinic?" he said, looking up from his notes.

"Yes, but, Doctor, I insist that you see this." Mom handed him the letter and waited.

The doctor took it and read it out loud: "'I agree to be responsible for Shumin's safety. If she has any problem after the surgery, I, together with the clinic, will take care of her two children until they grow up. Signed...'" He looked at her. "What's this?" he said, pushing up his glasses. "Why should I sign this?"

"I have serious high blood pressure and almost died the first time I gave birth. The doctor in the county's central hospital told me I couldn't have major surgery. If you *insist* on doing the surgery, then sign this letter first. My brother—he's a lawyer in the people's court—told me this." It was an exaggerated version of the truth, but she used the moment to give him the official note from the hospital.

He read this, paused for a moment to think, then turned to the nurse standing beside his desk. "Can you leave us for a few minutes? And take the kid!" he yelled, pointing at me.

When she came over to get me, I threw a tantrum. Like my mom, I was also refusing to do as I was told, and used all my strength to cry and kick the nurse away.

"Okay, never mind!" The doctor waved the nurse away. He studied the letter for a few more minutes and then glowered again at my mom. "I can't sign this, of course."

"Well, then, I can't lie on your table," she said, pointing to the gurney.

"You have to."

"Doctor, I really can't," she said, sounding composed. "Otherwise, I would have, long ago." She stared at him intensely. "Unless you sign the letter..."

The nurse returned. "It's hot outside; people are getting impatient. We have to go faster."

The doctor shouted at her to wait. He sat silently for a while as Mom held me.

Finally, he said very quietly: "Leave."

Mom didn't say a word; she just picked me up and left. Behind her, she heard him tell the nurse to bring in the next woman.

*   *   *

Some villagers found it suspicious. Shumin looked healthy as before, did not have to spend any time recovering in bed, and returned to the fields the same week after the "surgery."

"Shumin must have some powerful relatives," the villagers whispered.

Mom was probably one of very few women in the county with two children who did not have the operation. According to the Ministry of Health, each year—from 1983 to 2015—more than a million Chinese women were sterilized. In 1983 alone, the year China first implemented the One-Child Policy, more than 16 million women were forced to undergo surgery. The operation rooms—mostly temporary tents like the one my mom and I were taken to—were filthy, underequipped, and understaffed. The "surgeons" were often masked village doctors ordered to fulfill the urgent mission but who lacked the formal training to do so. Chronic pain and mental trauma haunted these women. Many of them were farmers who were subsequently no longer able to do strenuous manual work, and became dependent on a lifelong supply of painkillers they could barely afford. In many other ways, too, the surgeries had devastating consequences, especially for rural families. According to Chinese scholars who conducted field research in villages of ten provinces in 1995, 10 percent of China's rural women suffered from health problems caused by forced abortions and sterilization surgeries.

Mom felt lucky, or more in control of her own fate, so

she made another bold decision: to return to teaching. Her "victory" in giving birth to me and protecting her body from the government had increased her confidence: If she tried, nobody, not even her father-in-law or the government authorities, could stop her from what she understood to be her human rights. Going forward, she would be the one to decide how she would live her life.

She knew there were opportunities since Communist paramount leader Deng Xiaoping had launched "Reform and Opening Up" in 1978 to stimulate the economy, which made the prospect of owning a private business very attractive. Every month, Mom would hear of a teacher resigning in the hope of trying his or her luck at starting a new venture. Before Reform and Opening Up, all businesses were owned by the state. The government had banned private trading and labeled the independent entrepreneurs as trouble, alleging that their capitalist mind-sets and behaviors would pollute the purity of our country. If caught, they faced prison terms or even the death penalty. But the spring breeze of Reform and Opening Up melted the suppression of entrepreneurship. In the closest town, Lutai, although the state-owned businesses were still there, a new market was built to welcome privately run businesses, which quickly replaced those run by the state. The business owners, mostly in their twenties and thirties, were hip, ambitious risk-takers. They played pop songs from Hong Kong and Taiwan at their stalls, where they sold things like clothes, fruit, electronics, and CDs, which helped create a cool atmosphere.

The state-owned business operators resented the upstarts' newfound riches and sense of freedom. But this didn't stop people from wanting in, including those with government jobs or teachers, who quit to try their hands at making their own way alongside others from all walks of life. My parents were not used to taking such risks, but Mom was attracted to the idea of taking fate into your own hands, and now there would be more full-time teaching opportunities.

As they were finding their way, I had to stay with Nainai, which I hated. She smoked and would spend hours in the afternoon playing mahjong with other old people, who also smoked. I had difficulty breathing in such rooms, but Nainai was too distracted to pay any attention to me. At the mahjong table, Nainai fixed her eyes on her opponents' tiles, as if she could see through the cream glaze and know what was on the other side. She kept her ears just as sharp. The only good times I remember having with Nainai were when she was with another old lady, Grandma Liu, whose granddaughter, Mengmeng, was my good friend and lived in the house opposite ours. Mengmeng was also a second child but, unlike me, she had an elder sister. According to the One-Child Policy, rural families with firstborn girls were allowed to have a second child. The authorities understood a farmer's need for a son. No one had a retirement plan beyond relying on the younger generation's continuation of the work, and whose traditional duty was to look after their elders.

Though Mengmeng's birth was legal, her parents had made no announcement, aiming to try again for a son. They had a son when Mengmeng was two, and registered him in the *hukou* system instead of her.

The Chinese preference for boys dates back over two thousand years. The Chinese philosopher, Mencius (described as the "Second Sage" or second to Confucius himself), said that failure to produce an heir is the worst thing a dutiful (or filial) child could do. But the term he used referred to male children. In addition, people—like the villagers in Chaoyang—could cite dozens of reasons why boys were better:

Boys carry your family name.

Boys support you financially when you get old.

Boys sweep your tomb after you've passed away.

(Yes, this last one was relayed to me as a valid reason—as if girls cannot sweep!)

A more pragmatic reason was always that boys could get better jobs and could therefore earn more money. If the firstborn were a girl, there was still a chance for a boy to follow. But a second girl? Folks were not tolerant. They would either give away the second girl, or throw her away, literally. Mothers would spend hours praying to the Buddha and Taoist priests to bless them with a baby boy. If they had money or a good relationship with the hospital, some would pay the doctor or nurses extra money to check the gender of the fetus and abort females. Scholars believe that 30 to 60 million girls "disappeared" because of the One-Child Policy.

Mengmeng was a cheerful girl who always wore her hair in two braids, with red bows at the ends. She was five years old, one year older than me. She behaved like an older sister, wiping my tears and kissing my chubby face when I cried. When our grandmothers sat under the tree, chatting, sewing quilts, and hand-washing clothes in a wooden basin, Mengmeng and I were free to indulge ourselves in our own kingdom. We caught grasshoppers and kept them in a cage made from cornstalks; we dragged bamboo poles from the warehouse and used these to pick reddish dates from the tree we'd often sit under; we tied my mother's scarves around our waists like long dresses and mimicked the women in soap operas. The backyard was our secret garden. From here we could see the farmers under their straw hats; mothers stringing red peppers and corncobs, hanging them out to dry; grandparents chaperoning grand-children home after school; and the neighborhood yellow dog chasing cats and chickens up the road.

One day, when we were picking flowers in the yard and stirring them in dishes, pretending to "cook," Mengmeng looked lost in thought. When I tugged her arms to play, I noticed her eyes were red. I asked what was wrong.

"My parents are going to give me away," she said.

"What? Why?"

"I don't know. They are going to give me away and pre-tend they never had me." Mengmeng started to sob. "Don't tell anyone."

Her parents were not certain they could guarantee their son a *hukou* if the authorities knew about Mengmeng's ex-istence. My heart pounded hard in my chest again. *What if she is sent away? What if this happened to me?*

One afternoon, Nainai led me to Mengmeng's house as usual. Grandma Liu opened the door, her little grandson standing beside her. When she saw me, the old woman casually told me that Mengmeng wouldn't be home for a while but would come back soon. I knew she was lying. "You can play with Huanhuan today." She pulled my hand to her grandson's.

"No, I don't want to play with him," I declared. "I'll play by myself." It hurt to know that Mengmeng might never come back. I wanted to scream at her to return my friend.

That day, I quietly walked around alone, picking grass and flowers. I held the small basket of little pans and bowls in my hand that Mengmeng and I used to cook in. I sat down far from the little boy. Nainai sat under a willow tree with Grandma Liu, shelling peas.

"We heard that the birth-control officials will come again tomorrow," said Grandma Liu. "It's better to send her to her maternal grandparents' home for now, and see what happens." She used one sleeve to wipe the sweat dripping from her forehead. She was in her fifties, but her face looked as if it belonged to a woman who had had enough. Like Nainai, she was always plainly dressed. Their clothes consisted of four drab colors: black, gray, blue, and sometimes white in the summer. Women of her generation were used to wearing such simple clothes, a habit from Mao's era. On the rare occasions when she wore a colorful dress, her neighbors would gossip about her. For a long time, whenever I thought of a grandmother, I pictured a woman in plain cotton clothes.

Grandma Liu added, "Mengmeng's a bright girl. It's a pity. But a boy is what our family needs."

Mengmeng came back that winter. She did get a *hukou*, but only after her younger brother had been registered. Before that, whenever someone from the Birth Control Office came for the regular checkups, her parents would hide her somewhere and make her invisible.

*   *   *

I, too, was always aware that I was the different one. Growing up in the years when the One-Child Policy was most strictly enforced, I found it difficult to ignore that I was a second child. Although it took years for me to understand, I was sensitive to how people addressed me as "the second." Whenever I heard people calling me "the second," I would turn my head, pretending I didn't know what they were talking about. No matter how friendly they were, I disliked them after that.

Government officials referred to the One-Child Policy as "birth planning." I didn't understand what the officials came for, but I knew that whenever they did come to the village, it was not good. All we knew was that they would take away pregnant women and leave their child crying at the gate. The officials—who would rush in with wooden sticks—invaded and looted the homes of families who didn't pay the fine for their second child. No one would speak out against them. Some people were in agreement with the law, others were not.

It scared me, not only because of what was happening to my neighbors and those I knew, but also because I had come to believe that I could be taken away at any time. I'd slip into the haystack in my backyard, where I could hide but still see outside to the gate. I remember hiding there one day, watching a gray spider hunt winged insects on

the web it had spun on the elm tree beside me. I closed
my eyes and drifted asleep, but it didn't take long before
Nainai found me and dragged me out for dinner. "Get out
of there," she shouted. "Why did you put yourself in that
rabbit hole? Look at your dirty clothes." Nainai used her
apron to clean my face. "Policemen will come and take you
away if you don't behave."

I cried a lot as a child, and was most afraid of the police.
Whenever Yunxiang and I fought or if I cried about my
dolls being taken from me, Nainai would put a stop to it by
suggesting that the police would come and get me. I knew
the police had all the power and we had none, so I should
stay away from them.

Powerful people made Nainai nervous too.

Like everybody from their generation, Wengui and Nainai
worried a lot and easily. During their formative years, even
private conversations could cause serious trouble. After Mao's
death, when Reform and Opening Up brought more freedom
to the country, my grandparents and their peers had to learn
to forget the old dogmatic culture and they tried to relax. However, in 1983, three years of what is known as "Strike Hard"
began. Once again a powerful police state returned.

The Strike-Hard Campaign began when a group of party
leaders decided there was a need to restore public order. In
the 1950s, according to propaganda, it was so peaceful that it
was unnecessary to lock one's door at night. Leaders began to
believe the justice departments had been too soft on crime.
So, in summer 1983, Deng Xiaoping—the "paramount leader"
of China from 1978 to 1989 who led the country through far-
reaching economic reforms—launched a crime-fighting cam-

paign. Within a year of the start of this campaign, 861,000 people were tried in the criminal courts nationwide and 24,000 were sentenced to death. Petty thieves were sentenced to life. imprisonment, or even death. Young men were sentenced to death for dating and having sex with different women.

On a government-owned farm a mile from Chaoyang, people from nearby would sneak into the field to steal apples, corn, and whatever was growing that season. Nobody paid attention to this type of theft until the Strike-Hard Campaign. One young man was caught and sentenced to three years in prison for picking five ears of corn.

In the midst of such uncertainty, villagers in Chaoyang grasped onto an ancient rule: Silence is golden. To Nainai, to even say the name of Deng Xiaoping became taboo. I couldn't understand it, and, as a four-year-old, I enjoyed playing tricks on her by repeating things she had forbidden me from saying.

I surprised her one day by asking: "Will Mengmeng be given away?"

"She's safe now."

"Will I be given away?"

She burst into laughter. "You're too expensive." Nainai always called me a "costly girl," and it made me feel guilty. I did not know why it was funny, and my expression said so.

"Maybe. If you don't behave well," she added. Nainai pulled me over to face Grandma Liu. "In our time, who would have spent so much for a girl?"

"Girls are born to be unlucky," Nainai mumbled as she plucked a piece of reed and folded the flat, boat-shaped leaves into a pinwheel for me.

I nodded, not sure if I understood. I held the pinwheel up high and ran along the edge of the pond.

Her words haunted me for a long time. Why did she value boys over girls, even though she was a girl? She died before I was old enough to ask her.

Nainai was orphaned at three years old and never went to school. Sadly, she was the sort of woman who did all the housework, but whom nobody ever bothered to thank. At night, she always sat under a dim lamp, darning our socks. She had cataracts, and worked with the needle so close to her eyes that I worried she would poke one of them out. This is one of the reasons why Nainai didn't get along well with my mom, who had career ambitions. As far as Nainai was concerned, my mom's teaching job would give our family a bad reputation. Nainai, who had five daughters herself but was considered lucky because she had two sons, always saved the fine rice and noodles for her husband and sons, while she and her daughters ate coarse bread made from corn flour.

She used to say that girls were useless. I hated this, but eventually managed to melt the icy barrier around her heart. One day, when I helped her to peel green beans and build a fire for dinner, she took a blue-and-white handkerchief from her gray cotton coat. In the handkerchief were hard candies. "Open your mouth!" she said, picking one piece out for me. "When my little girl grows up and marries someone with a lot of money, will you still remember Nainai and take care of me?"

"Yes, Nainai," I'd said. She couldn't imagine that I would ever be able to take care of her myself.

Many times after Mom would come home, I'd tell her that I didn't want to be taken by the police, or thrown into the dustbin like Nainai teased me. Mom would reassure me, holding me in her arms, and sing to me. Years later, I still hear this song in my dreams:

> The moon is bright, the wind quiet;
> The leaves' shadows fall on the windowsill;
> The crickets are crying, making sounds
> like stringed instruments;
> The music is soft, bright,
> The tone is pleasing;
> The cradle gently swings;
> My baby closes her eyes
> and dreams her sweet dreams.

I would always be happy in the evenings when everyone was finally at home after a long day's work, and Mom's singing always brought extra comfort. What I remember most vividly about being five years old in Chaoyang is the rain, when my parents and grandparents would stay home from work. I loved watching the water trickle down the glass and collect on the windowsill. Hooks, hanging from the sills, would sometimes blow in the wind, chiming softly. Those were the days I most enjoyed, and when I felt the safest. On those rainy days, I didn't worry about being taken.

CHAPTER THREE

A Home of Our Own

Caiyuan, 1995

In Chaoyang village, houses were connected to each other in a row without any space between them and always at the same height. To be polite, neighbors discussed the height of their homes before any renovation or construction, and if somebody planned for their house to be taller, it was not regarded well. There were also practical reasons for them to be the same height: Otherwise, if it rained, the water would collect on the roofs of the shorter homes and damage them over time.

My parents had finally built their own house next door to my grandparents—at the same height—but Mom and Wengui, whose relationship since my birth had reached a kind of uneasy peace, finally exploded when she refused to pay for a new house to celebrate my uncle's marriage. Wengui had insisted that the family come together to pay for Uncle's house, and because Wengui was still the head of the family, Baba and his siblings were expected to oblige. But Mom would not. She and my dad made their own money, and she believed it should be theirs to keep.

Their inflamed arguments over the proposed building lasted for a few months, and neither my mom nor Wengui would give in. Then, a few days before Chinese Lunar New Year, my grandfather announced that he was going ahead with construction, and that the new house would be in the same row and next to my parents', but three feet higher.

A few days after the festivities, when the sun hadn't fully risen, my mom and I were suddenly awoken by a drilling sound. When she opened the curtain, she saw two tractors pulling wagons filled with soil parked in front of my grand-father's house. Wengui stood in his yard, instructing the two drivers on how to lay foundations.

Mom quickly dressed and rushed out the door.

"Both are your sons," she yelled at him. "How can you be so unfair to us? We've only had our house for a few years. Why are you so evil?"

"You refused to talk to me about this," Wengui responded matter-of-factly and took a puff of his pipe, "so now I've done what I think is best."

Mom went into my grandparents' kitchen and sat down. Wengui walked over and stood in front of her. She began to hammer away at the details: "We paid for his college tu-ition. For years we've handed in half our earnings to you. Now we have a house but a lot of debt. I have treated Chengtai's sisters like my own. Tell me, what have we done wrong?"

If my mother had shown weakness by crying, like other women in the village when they wanted something, Wengui would have been less angry. But her strong will—her own ideas, opinions, her strength—was exactly what he didn't like about her.

"You know what's wrong"—Wengui raised his voice—"you never listen to us! You want to keep working as a teacher, yet you're a married woman. You had a second child, you don't wash my son's clothes, and now you encourage my son to turn his back on his family. If this were the old days, you would have been returned to your parents long ago!"

"But it's not the old days anymo—"

Before she could finish, Nainai came out from her room, shouting in her raspy voice, "Chengtai, if you don't control your wife, you're not my son anymore! Who is this woman? She shows no respect to us!" She then sat on the ground and cried over and over again, "I will die today. Chengtai, if you don't teach your wife a lesson, I will die today!"

My mother stood up and kicked the chair toward Nainai. The glasses and teapots crashed to the floor. She slammed the door and rushed out, yelling, "I can't live near you people anymore."

"Stop, woman!" Wengui shouted. "Who permitted you to leave this house?"

Hearing his mother's wailing, my father ran inside. He first pulled up his mother from the floor. As he was about to walk out to my mother, Wengui hit him in the shoulder with his walking stick and shouted, "You pathetic son! You're going to her?"

The workers, still on the tractors, which by now had been switched off, looked at each other and didn't know what to do. Nainai was crying on a stool in front of the window. Neighbors stood around outside, enjoying the scene; family drama was the best entertainment a village could have. Otherwise there was just farming, cooking, and caring for children.

Mom came at Wengui with her fist. He grabbed her. She forcefully tried to free her hands to pound him and punch him, but he held on tightly and squeezed her so hard that it hurt. Four neighbors tried unsuccessfully to pull them apart.

In all the screaming, crying, and chaos, my father sneaked out through the yard.

By lunch, he had returned with his siblings and their spouses, but they only defended my grandparents, adding fuel to the flames.

Among the onlookers, an old man from my mother's village, who happened to be in Chaoyang selling candies on his bicycle, had seen the fight and sped back to inform my mother's family. Her siblings soon arrived to help. By midafternoon, there was no turning back.

To the neighbors watching, it didn't matter what the fight was about. A daughter-in-law disobeying the parents? She was wrong. Terrible. A monster. My mother knew this was not simply a matter of losing face. It meant she would not have a friend in the village tomorrow. The elders would despise her, and the young would be pressured to avoid associating with her.

That day in the chaos, I ran from here to there in our yard and then sneaked out and sat on the street until the evening. When people passed over me, talking, I suspected they were whispering about all the craziness in my yard. I kept my face buried in my arms so they couldn't see I was Shumin's daughter.

Suddenly my mother's older brother Shouchun appeared in front of me and told me to get in his car, where my mother and Yunxiang sat waiting. Uncle Shouchun drove us to Caiyuan. I knew it wasn't a usual visit to my other grandparents' because, on the way, my mother didn't say a word. Her swollen eyes remained fixed on the road for the entire drive.

My father did not come to Caiyuan that night, or the next one. He would not dare disagree with his father. It worried me. The sour relationship between Mom and Grandfather Wengui negatively affected my parents' marriage. I had heard the word *divorce* often from them both. After many days with no Baba I began to worry even more, and didn't want to leave either of them.

Eventually, after a few weeks when things calmed down, Baba came to see us. Initially he stayed only one night a week, then two nights, then three, until finally he moved in. That was my father's style. When he met with difficulty, he preferred to wait it out or escape rather than put himself in front of it. My mom would rather be run over by a truck than wait. With his way, Baba managed to keep the hearts of both sides, but his parents still blamed him for being disloyal, and his wife and children trusted him less.

We all remained living together in Caiyuan with my mother's parents. The two villages were close, and Yunxiang could still attend the same school. I liked the new village, playing with my cousin Chunting, and making new friends. Mom returned to teaching that year at her old school, and Baba continued driving his tractor to sell bricks and, now, also fertilizer. But they were unhappy. Baba would smoke in the yard for hours, and Mom's otherwise easy laughter had become rare. A married daughter returning home to live with her parents was a big no-no. Her parents tried to reassure Mom that she could stay as long as she wanted, never mind the busybodies, but the knowing looks and whispers whenever she walked by made Mom feel too self-conscious.

There is an old Chinese saying that a married daughter is like spilled water: "Once she is out, she is out." After marriage, the only times daughters were truly welcomed in their parents' homes were during a few major festivals or for weddings and funerals. It had been that way for many years. Customs and societal norms shift, but in the countryside in the 1990s married daughters seldom visited their parents, so a woman who returned too often was considered disrespectful to her in-laws.

What's more, my mother's fight with her in-laws had been public; only a delirious or insane woman would openly challenge her father-in-law.

Then, to make matters even worse, Grandfather Wengui died of cancer a few months after we had moved out.

And so my mother's sins doubled in the eyes of his friends and relatives. His medical records said he had succumbed to lung cancer, but they were sure he had died of humiliation and anger at my mother.

We went to Grandfather Wengui's funeral, all of us dressed in traditional white from head to toe. Baba's siblings refused to talk to Mom. My aunt insisted that I follow her closely and not walk with my mother to the cemetery.

Many Kans whom I had never met attended. A band of musicians followed the long procession of mourners and played gongs, trumpets, and drums. I looked for my mom the entire time; she was always at the front of the line. As the wife of the deceased's oldest son, Mom was expected to cry all the way to the cemetery, whether she missed him or not. She also had to hold a pottery bowl filled with the ashes of "ghost money"—fake bills printed with images of the gods, which when burned would be used in the afterlife. She had to scatter the ashes at the entrance to the village. I knew Wengui would be happy to see Mom giving away the "cash" in his honor. He managed to win, even in death.

As we approached his coffin, I grew especially scared. Spooky characters from traditional Chinese tales were embroidered on the decorative cloth covering the coffin. There were gods' messengers with their green faces, and the judge who decided whether somebody would be sent to heaven or hell, surrounded by long-eared black ghosts. The entire funeral freaked me out.

I was happy when evening arrived and the sun settled into sleep. At night, before the actual burial the next day, it is customary to play music in front of the deceased's home. When the music played, it felt as if the entire village was in our yard for Wengui's send-off. We stood around drinking soda and watching a female singer belt out pop songs. It was bizarre to me that she had chosen such happy music. I asked Mom about it, and she said if an old man died in bed, it was a blessing and deserved celebration. I started to think about how I would never see my grandfather again, and I cried. However grumpy he was, I missed him. He was always smoking and worried, but I still loved him. Though I could not let Mom see me cry, for I feared she'd feel betrayed.

★　★　★

Despite my friendship with Mengmeng, my cousin Chunting was more like the sister I had always wanted. She and I were always together—sleeping, eating, playing, and watching TV. But as much as I liked Caiyuan, I knew it was not my home. In the villages, family names mattered more than blood. Chinese culture differentiates the children of sons from the children of daughters. Because Yunxiang and I didn't share the same family name with Laoye, my mother's father, we were his *waisun*, meaning his "outer-grandchildren," while Chunting, Uncle Lishui's daughter, was a *neisun*, an "inner-grandchild." It was in our grandparents' best interest to focus on and take care of the *neisuns* first; we *waisuns* were always second. My mother hated to burden her parents with caring for Yunxiang and me, and didn't want to cause arguments between her parents and sisters-in-law.

My mother warned Yunxiang and me that, when she was not around, we were to behave as best as we could. We were never to fight with our uncles' children, and were to try not to eat at our uncles' houses. If we needed pocket money, we were never to ask our uncles or grandparents. If our socks or gloves were torn, we were to wait for Mom to fix them, and not ask my grandmother.

Uncle Lishui teased Mom, and said she was thinking too much about it. "You sound like one of these paranoid old ladies," he said, but my mother insisted that since we were living in her parents' village, it was best to be careful and avoid more trouble.

The villagers did not openly give Mom a hard time, but they didn't hide their opinions either. One day as I was walking in the street with Chunting to my uncle's house, we met a group of grannies sitting on the curb in front of the village chief's office, in an open area used for hanging out. With nothing better to do, these old ladies spent most of their time getting into other people's business. One narrow-eyed old woman pointed out Chunting to the other ladies. "That girl is Lishui's daughter, but who's the one beside her?" She waved her hands to Chunting, beckoning her. "Come here!"

Chunting and I looked at each other, then obediently went over to them.

Another lady, a little younger, said: "This one is Shumin's daughter. You know Shumin? Lishui's sister who had the fight with her in-laws?"

"Ah," they said. One turned her head to me and said with a sneering smile, "You don't belong here. Why are you here all the time?"

The group laughed. To them it was harmless teasing, but I took it seriously. I was angry, but too shy to argue back. I bit my lip and lowered my head, avoiding eye contact. I hated these awful old women with their loose yellow teeth and gray clothes. I pulled Chunting's sleeve and could still hear them laughing as we walked away.

In the evening when my mom came back from school, I told her about what had happened.

"Don't listen to them," she said too simply. I didn't understand why she kept quiet about people teasing us, and why she seemed extra anxious lately. Even the music she used to like now bothered her. Her tape collection gathered dust on the shelves and she had stopped singing around the house.

Her status in Caiyuan was not easy for her to accept emotionally, but she had to live with it. It wasn't the snickering women who bothered her though. What really disturbed my mother was living with what she had done to me.

In Caiyuan, many parents did not put much into their children's education. They had neither money nor high expectations. Farming was the priority. To most of them, sending their kids to school was merely a way to keep them busy and out of trouble. Many of the children didn't even finish the first nine years of education the government provided for free. Only a few would make it to high school. If a child went to college, it was such big news that the whole village celebrated. One year when a boy was accepted to Tsinghua University, one of the best schools in China, he received a 10,000-yuan cash award from the local government. A band of trumpets and drums played in front of his home, and a big flower necklace made of lucky red-colored cloth was placed around his neck.

My mother was worried that raising us in such a rural environment would be detrimental to our future.

Yunxiang's behavior was also ratcheting up her anxiety. At eleven years old, he played hooky and sat in video gaming bars. In the dim huts, renovated storerooms along the national road leading to the neighboring province, a few sets of screens connected to Nintendo 64 accessories had been installed against the wall. Kids, still wearing their schoolbags, sat on chairs, unmoving, staring at screens on which animated characters fought and moved under their direction. Most villagers did not mind; Nintendo 64 was a sign of modernity and progress. "The Japanese are evil, but they are so damn good at technology," they'd say. A friend of Yunxiang, whose father was the best carpenter in the county and was thus richer than most, bought the consoles to play at home.

Yunxiang and I were regularly invited to gaming parties, where the host would show off their wares: *Contra*, *Battle City*, and *Super Mario*. But Mom hated the games. She said our time could be better spent. She would ground us every time she caught us coming out of the gaming bars. I spent a few evenings inside every month, but Yunxiang was grounded every week. One of our cousins, Chunheng, dropped out of school at fifteen to be a gamer, and Yunxiang had looked up to him like an older brother.

When my mother asked Uncle Lishui why he was okay with his son not going to school, he laughed.

"Someone has to farm. Otherwise, how would we survive? Don't worry, he'll be fine, he won't starve."

Uncle Lishui made a good living buying glass wholesale and selling it from the back of a three-wheel cart at a marked-up price in nearby villages.

"But don't you want more for him? Look at our brother Shoukui; he's a lawyer, in Lutai. Don't you want something like that for Chunheng?"

"Shumin, you think too much—that's why you're so unhappy!" Uncle teased. "Our children have their own lives, and their own fate." He patted her on the back. "If you really care so much, why don't you move to Lutai?"

Uncle Lishui's flippant response gave her an idea. Why not move to Lutai? Mom knew there was no hope for her to be promoted as a registered teacher, since she'd had a second child and that broke the law. She was tired of being a substitute teacher. If we moved there, where no one knew us, the past would be the past. We'd make a new home and a fresh start. Uncle Shoukui was already there, and his two sons were good students. What's more, the schools were better there: They taught more than just Chinese and mathematics. They also had music and art classes, and sports. Mom decided that, more than ever, we needed to be living in a town, instead of in a small village. She didn't know how we would manage without a job or a plan, but she knew it was the sort of life she wanted for us.

The town of Lutai and our village were only six miles apart, but towns had government jobs, and the children attended modern schools. If we moved, it would cost us: We'd have to pay rent and other bills like water, which was free in our village, and electricity. Although primary school, grades one through nine, were free, to have after-school activities like art and music classes required an additional fee.

More money was what Mom needed, but didn't have. It was already difficult to make ends meet. But she decided the move would be worth it. She knew of people who had moved from other provinces and managed to settle down well in town. Why couldn't she?

The greatest obstacle was the *hukou*, which strictly controlled and facilitated the rules of internal migration. The *hukou* system began in ancient China, when the emperors wanted to prevent free migration. When Sun Yat-sen and the Nationalist Party founded China's first republic in 1912 after the Qing dynasty was overthrown, they promised to end such restrictions. The Republic of China's first constitution in 1912 acknowledged freedom of movement as a human right. The Chinese Communist Party upheld that right for the first few years, and then they began to change their minds.

A decade after the People's Republic was founded, Sino-Soviet relations soured. The Soviets threatened China's border and the fractured relationship worsened the already frosty international environment for China. A new plan was put into place, requiring rural residents to remain with the land to ensure food production; thus, the *hukou* system was reinstated in an effort to balance a number of people working in factories against those working in the fields. Citizens had to register their age, gender, marital status, and, most importantly, their hometown. After 1958, moving from village to city was not allowed unless the government approved.

Migration became less tightly controlled after Reform and Opening Up in 1978. But the right to migrate freely never returned to China's constitution.

Where you could work and where you could get married, as well as whether you received a good education, health care, or a pension, were all determined by *hukou*, and urban workers had it better than farmers.

This unfair, discriminatory system exists today, enshrined by law.

Hukou meant that, because I was born in a village, I was deemed inferior to anyone born in a city, no matter how much harder I worked or how much more deserving I might be. It was disheartening as a child because all the adults in my life also instilled in me that *hukou* mattered. As an immigrant, you become an alien in a new land; to feel like an alien in your own country is another matter.

For the rural villagers, entering a town would have felt as magical as stepping into Oz, or into Daguanyuan, the mansion in one of the most famous Chinese novels, the *Dream of the Red Chamber*. In towns, the streets were all paved, so on rainy days mud would not ruin your trousers; the residents rode bikes to their factory jobs every morning and did not have to walk for miles; workers wore tidy blue uniforms with turned-up white collars; the floors of their homes were covered in clean gray tiles, not dirty bricks.

My mother would never forget the first time she visited her relatives in town. Before they let her in, they handed her a pair of slippers at the door. She was momentarily at a loss for words; then she realized no one in town wore their dust-covered shoes inside. This was my mother's first impression of Lutai. She felt inferior, like a fish out of water.

My parents knew they could not simply leave the village and take up the good life in town so easily. It would be nearly impossible for her or my father to get urban *hukous*.

The only way a status change could happen is if someone went to college and secured a government job, as my oldest uncle, Shoukui, had done.

So my mother could not rely on government support, and there were no job openings, not even for manual labor. It was 1996, and there were only three state-owned factories—a cotton mill, a steel mill, and a frozen seafood-processing plant—which were all doing terribly and rumored to be on the brink of shutting down. It was no secret that the cotton mill had been losing money for years, and that workers at the seafood-processing factory had work only three days a week because of decreasing demand from their main Japanese client, who switched their business to another privately owned factory in Dalian that worked faster than Lutai's state-owned one. The old model of state-owned companies was facing a crisis nationwide—once drivers of the economy, they were now being reformed, privatized, or shut down.

Private enterprise became more and more important after Deng Xiaoping's Reform and Opening Up, but core, state-owned enterprises still had no real competition.

Government-employed factory workers enjoyed stable, low-pressure jobs; productivity remained low and management rigid. When Premier Zhu Rongji came to power in the 1990s, he targeted the then-bloated state-owned enterprises that employed so many, yet produced so little. Millions lost their jobs in the ten years following. In small towns like Lutai, the state-owned enterprises were dying, but the private ones didn't arrive to replace them—they preferred to be in cities first. There were too few jobs in town even for those with urban *hukous*. And Lutai residents topped the long waiting lists for work.

Mom thought first about using their little savings to start a business in the New Market. She'd rent a shop to sell fruit, seafood, and flowers. But what did she know about running a business? She had neither the experience nor the mind-set to survive the competition.

Weeks passed, and Mom began to give up hope. "We might be stuck in Caiyuan Village forever," she'd tell me sadly. I was sad too. I didn't want to be in a place where people whispered about me, but I also didn't want to leave Chunting and my grandparents. Then Uncle Shoukui visited with good news: his wife had recently opened a kindergarten, but the loud, out-of-control town kids were too much for her to handle. Why didn't my mother take it over?

Mom did not know if she could handle it, either, but her years of teaching made her well qualified, and Baba could help her. He had a high school diploma, a rarity that would add credibility to their venture. My dad was not sold on the idea, but he supported her, as he always did. Contrary to the custom, by now he had become used to being a helper in our family rather than the decision-maker. I suspect other families had a similar dynamic, though none would dare admit it.

The state-funded kindergartens in town were too few and their teachers were known to be too lazy—or so parents complained: too much time painting pretty pictures, not enough time practicing characters.

In urban China, where the competition begins on day one, parents did not want their children playing with their friends; they wanted them learning. And they did not want to pay the one hundred yuan per month that state-run schools charged for something they considered little better than babysitting. Private kindergartens had fewer textbooks and supplies, but they made up for the lack of resources by being just about affordable, and by focusing on core subjects such as math and writing.

We were among the first families from all the dozens of villages in Ninghe County to leave and move to a town. Chinese people have a deep attachment to the land. Traditionally, people believed they should remain on the land where they were born until the day they died. As a farmer, you were born on the land, grew up on the same land, and one day, if you were a man, you were buried in that land. Your ancestors were there, and your descendants would follow. Only promises of great fortune or calamity could entice people to leave—a catastrophic event like a famine or flood, or the opportunity to sit on an official throne.

But I was nervous about moving again. It had been less than two years since we moved from Chaoyang to Caiyuan. I was seven, and didn't care about a good education or paved roads. All I cared about were my friends. *Are people in Lutai nice? Will I meet new friends? Will they want to chase fireflies with me? Will there be enough stars in the town's sky?* I had many questions and concerns, but Mom said moving was the right thing to do. I had no choice but to trust her.

CHAPTER FOUR

We, the Migrants in Town

Lutai, 1996

Lutai is also known as Reed Island. Towns and villages with *tai* and *gu* in their names—both words for "island"—were everywhere in Tianjin, where five rivers funneled into the sea through the mouth of the Hai River. It created scores of tiny landmasses between crisscrossing waterways. Reeds shrouded Lutai's streams, rivers, and ponds. As tall as a grown man, the reeds were felled in the autumn and dried in the sun to make *baolian*, thick mats used to insulate roofs. The reeds in Lutai had a reputation for being more waterproof than average, and were also used to weave mats to pad chairs and beds, as well as baskets for storing food. They brought wealth to the town, enticing many to live there.

When not weaving, Lutai's residents would fish. Old people said they could catch enough fish, crabs, and shellfish for a day's meal within a few short hours using nothing but homemade nets. Lutai's two-inch silvery whitebait was famous for being tender and tasty. Big-city restaurants would buy it by the crate. When they had sold all they could, the fish were dried and saved for winter. But that was before I was born. Since the late 1980s, the water gradually became polluted, and fishermen had a much harder time making ends meet.

As the Chinese saying goes: "A sparrow may be tiny, but its body is complete." Though Lutai was a small town, its population outgrew the number the government once planned for it when the new China was founded and the town rebuilt. A centrally orchestrated economy was introduced in the mid-1950s, modeled after the Soviet Union. The government calculated how much the country would consume each year, and formulated a plan to produce the amount to meet the estimate. The government also allocated set-wage jobs to workers based on their skills. Consumer goods—from rice and pork to soap and bicycles—were rationed. Lutai's planners, like their colleagues in other towns around the country, expected their citizens to stay put, as dictated. Facilities and infrastructure were installed for about fifty thousand people, and no more. There was one police station, one cinema, one park, one state-owned market, and two hospitals—one each for traditional Chinese and Western medicine. Today, more than 130,000 people live in Lutai. I grew up after Reform and Opening Up, so my generation has always taken for granted the abundance of resources, products, and big shopping malls. I could not imagine having to bathe using a slivered ration of soap. My parents and grandparents weren't so lucky.

However, even with the old days long gone, in the nineties, the stains of that bullish economy remained.

When we arrived in Lutai, a business-driven urbaniza-tion had begun and was booming. People were taking their fate into their own hands. Street peddlers sold steamed buns, soy milk, and eggs pickled in tea from illegal street stands. The two-story Workers' Club was now filled with sellers peddling cheap clothes and pirated books. Locals complained about all the migrants with weird accents run-ning businesses and selling suspicious foreign products: cigarettes from Taiwan, beers from Vietnam, and fur hats from Russia, all of which were probably imported illegally. In life, change occurs every day, but the shift is sometimes so incremental it's imperceptible. The locals complained about the migrants who rushed into the town and sold ille-gally imported or fake products, migrants who made their streets dirty and messy; but no matter how much they com-plained, they still bought the cheap pots, knives, shampoos, and shoes from migrants.

At seven, I was wide-eyed when we arrived in Lutai. It was so modern. Every Tuesday afternoon, Baihua Cinema would announce a new film by papering a Hollywood poster on its gray cement wall. The courthouse, police bureau, and tax bureau each had their own buildings in the center of town. Two yuan would get you a whole day in Fangzhou Park, where there were paddleboats and pink lotus alongside the riverbank. The newly built Fuli Hotel featured Lutai's first swimming pool and seafood buffet. The Luyang shopping mall was the tallest, with six floors and a clock on top. I liked to look up at it each time I passed. The shopping mall had everything a village child could imagine. I wanted to wear the little white dress with red polka dots that I saw in a shop window and to taste the chocolate bars wrapped in paper printed with Russian *matryoshka*.

We moved into a traditional single-story house in the *hutongs*, the narrow alleys commonly found in the old section of northern Chinese cities. It was a rental apartment in a community called Dongdaying, or the East Barrack, once reserved for the military during the Qing dynasty. I was disappointed as soon as I saw it. It was not like the fancy new homes we had seen advertised on the sides of buses as we drove through town. The homes in Dongdaying were run down, and had been built in the 1970s. The streets, though paved, were full of holes. The alleys were too narrow for two cars to pass, so one car would have to wait at the corner for the other. Wires running from the telephone poles were tangled like spiderwebs along the edges of homes. Our walls were so paper thin that at dinner I could hear the clash of spatula on pans and smell the frying vegetables from next door. How was this the "bright future" Mom had promised? We slept in a small room together, whereas Yunxiang and I had our own bedrooms back home. I didn't understand how Mom could prefer this over the village. I didn't understand what made the town better, except the tall buildings and lavish shops we couldn't afford.

The shabby *hutong* neighborhood was not comfortable, nor was it safe.

One day a rainstorm brought down the power lines on our street. No one had inspected the lines in years, and the frayed cable ends fell into a puddle, electrocuting a man. When his wife tried to save him, she died too. When the policemen came to take the bodies, I sat inside and could still hear the family's wailing over the blaring sirens. From then on, I always walked on the far right side of our street, away from the power lines.

Our home had four rooms and a small yard. The walls were lime-washed, and if I touched them, my fingers would end up covered in white powder. The iron windows were rusted. The floor was cement, and the kitchen was furnished with only a shelf and a large blue tin filled with liquefied natural gas used for cooking. Every few months when it was emptied, Baba would pay thirty-five yuan to refill it at a gas station.

My parents hadn't brought any furniture with them, so we had very little in our home. For many years, I never brought classmates home, and turned down invitations to visit theirs. I couldn't bear to have to reciprocate, and reveal how we lived.

The summer was hot and humid in Lutai, and afternoon showers regularly flooded the poorly drained streets. This made the *hutongs* a breeding ground for mosquitoes. When I forgot to apply repellent, my arms and legs would be covered with bites within minutes. Baba had to climb a ladder onto the roof every day to check for leaks. If he didn't get there in time, the rain could drip through to the walls. Mom used the empty laundry basin to collect the water dripping from the ceiling. I'd sit counting the drops per minute to try to cheer myself up.

Outside, our flooded yard would take days to dry. Tree roots blocked the drainpipe. My father and our next-door neighbor, Old Chen, once dug up the whole road in an attempt to clear the drains, but by the next week, the floods were back. The inside of our home sometimes became so damp that it smelled unrelentingly of mold, which made me feel sick to my stomach. When the sun came out, I'd run quickly to hang my laundered shirts on a string tied between two trees. Those days were always a relief, and the sunshine reminded me of my village.

When we moved in, Old Chen and his wife, Aunt Cui, came over to welcome us. The couple, both in their early fifties, were the unofficial chiefs of the neighborhood. Old Chen had a pale, round face, and wore a hat no matter the season. He was a real city man who had come to Lutai from the Tianjin city center in the sixties as part of Mao's campaign to educate urban youth by sending them to rural areas to "experience hardship" and contribute to reconstructing the countryside. They were referred to as the "sent-down youth." He met and married Cui in Lutai. After Mao's death, they chose to stay, unlike the tens of millions of other sent-down youths who returned to their cities.

Aunt Cui, a plump woman with short, well-coiffed hair, was the closest Lutai had to aristocracy. The daughter of Communist Party cadres, she was revered not because she had contributed much or achieved anything, but because she came from a wealthy family. She and her siblings worked in government offices. The Cuis could afford a more expensive apartment in town, but they, along with their extended family, preferred to dominate and rule in the old neighborhood, where they had lived for decades.

They planned to send their second daughter to college in America. "It's expensive there," Cui said. "A meal in the US

costs more than a whole week's meals here." I knew nothing about America except that the people were big and had
different eye colors, as I had seen in films.

*Maybe because of their size they have to eat a lot, and
that's why a meal is so expensive,* I thought.

While Lao Chen and Aunt Cui lived next door, her
brother and parents lived in the row opposite our house.
Across the street in another *hutong* lived Wang Jianli and
his family.

Wang Jianli was a wiry man in his late thirties. He and
his family lived in a four-room house with a small yard,
inherited from his parents, who in turn had been given
the home by their employers, a state-owned factory. Wang
Jianli had a small confectionary shop, but his wife took care
of it most of the time. He spent his time chatting and playing chess.

Next door to Wang Jianli lived the Li family from Hunan
Province, over nine hundred miles away. The Lis were small
and had tanned skin. They rented three rooms out of an otherwise abandoned factory nearby, which they had set up as a
bakery. Their son, Li Chun, was the same age as I was, and
had big eyes and yellowish hair, which tickled me.

Even at a young age, I quickly worked out the neighborhood hierarchy. The Cui family was always in the right. No
matter man or woman, young or old, all the adults respect-
fully addressed the matriarch as Sister Cui or Aunt Cui. They
had built an extension to their house—a kitchen and bathroom next to their main rooms—on public property without
permission, but no one complained or asked that it be removed. The Li family was treated quite differently. When

they built a shelter outside in their yard, the authorities quickly called it illegal and within weeks came to tear it down.

When the Cuis' younger daughter, Lan, was studying for her college-entrance exam, Wang Jianli and his friends would stop their rants about international affairs under the poplar tree to beam at her with joy whenever she passed, and wish her luck on the test. Yet they never worried about disturbing us during my and Yunxiang's naptime. I wanted Mom or Baba to shout at them to be quiet, but Baba said, as newcomers, it was important to build a good relationship with our neighbors.

"Even when they're not nice?" I protested from our room. But Mom said it was the price we had to pay as migrants.

Neither we nor the Lis were locals, and the Wangs, who regarded themselves as real Lutai folks, treated us differently. They treated the Lis worse, because they had come from farther away.

Wang and his gang were sometime merciless, mocking the Li family's Hunan accents—which caused them to mispronounce "shi" as "si" and "n" as "l"—and referred to them as "the southern barbarians" behind their backs. The Lis' way of speaking was novel to me too: I had never heard a southern accent. But I saw no reason to make fun of it. Like us, they were trying hard to get by, and always spoke Mandarin. They'd struggle to find the correct words at times. Their Mandarin was not perfect, but neither was my other neighbors'.

I liked playing with Li Chun much better than the local Lutai kids because he had better stories, which were different from mine.

He told me about how his father, a man who didn't talk much, had left his mother, his siblings, and him behind in Hunan for two years so he could work construction in Tianjin. The money he earned in a month at the construction site was more than what he would earn in six months in his village. But he missed his family. His cousin got him a job in a bakery, where he worked day and night for six months. He studied every component of the operation until he mastered it: ingredients, oven temperatures, and baking times, learning which factory provided the best but cheapest flour, and calculating how many cakes a customer would need per month.

He figured out that his boss earned more than 5,000 yuan per month, and so, with money he had saved and borrowed, he started his own bakery. My mother admired the Lis for their courage, and unlike other parents in our neighborhood, she encouraged me to play with Li Chun. She said that Li was good at "bitter eating," a Chinese term to describe people who are hardworking.

Li Chun and I spent a lot of time playing in either the backyard of his parents' bakery or in the small, open space outside our own back door. In the bakery's empty yard, Li Chun liked to inspect grass and tree leaves, crawling around, looking for snails, and chasing cats that yowled in protest. One day I told him I had come to Lutai on a bus that took forty minutes. He said the train that had brought him took more than a day.

"You're lying," I told him. "Trains don't go that long!" I had never been on a train.

"If I am lying, then may I turn into a little dog," Li Chun

said, grinning and mimicking a thirsty dog. I laughed. He also laughed, revealing a missing front tooth.

Li Chun told me his hometown, Hunan, was green even in the winter, and that his grandfather lived beside a bamboo forest. In his grandfather's magical hands, *poof*, bamboo became chairs.

"In Hunan," he said, "people lived in two-story houses. The first floor is for dining and storage, the second for bedrooms. For the Dragon Boat Festival, people race real 'dragon boats' on the river. The bow is shaped like a dragon's head," he went on, outlining the shape in the air. "It's not like here, where there's nothing."

I realize now that we exchanged these stories to escape our reality. No matter where we were from, being migrants felt like a trap.

Even after my parents were able to buy our house in the *hutong*, using money they had saved after two years added to the money they had borrowed from relatives and friends, we still did not fit in. Li Chun was my friend because we were alike—outcasts. We didn't have other friends and were largely ignored by our neighbors. The street committee, a form of local government, never bothered to tell our parents about policies or decisions that would affect us, as they would inform the other locals. Whether it was raising the sanitation fee or selecting delegates for the National People's Congress, we were kept in the dark. Many of the Lutai people believed we had come to take their jobs, and because of that we were made to be invisible. But I thought it was not all too bad. When they didn't like something, it was the Chinese way to pretend that it did not exist. It reminded me of Mengmeng, though I no longer feared being taken. Instead, Li Chun and I enjoyed sneaking around wherever we liked: Li's cake shop, the abandoned factory, the pond at the north end of the *hutong* where I could pick lotus. Nobody reported our whereabouts to our parents like people in the village would have done. Nobody teased me with their mean jokes. I simply did not matter. I was not one of them.

*   *   *

The locals had three favorite topics: how to get rich, the rumored *hutong* demolition, and President Jiang Zemin's love life. A few months after we moved to our *hutong*, there was talk of a demolition. The locals were excited about the prospect of being given new apartments as compensation by the government and developers, as had already happened in other neighborhoods. People loved the new apartments, which included indoor bathrooms and kitchens. But this caused anxiety for migrants like us. Even now that we owned our house, would the government treat us differently because of our rural *hukou*? Some people said the new apartments would be provided only to employees of the state-owned factories. But others said it was nonsense; every family, as long as they could provide the house's ownership certificate, would be treated the same. We had moved to a filthy place where we were ridiculed and looked down upon as if we were dogs, but it was the best life we could've hoped for. Mom did not want us to return to the village and farm for the rest of our lives. My parents had made a sacrifice and, though I despised the *hutongs*, I understood why it mattered that we remain there. No one knew the truth, our fates rested in the hands of the government, and we were left to wonder.

"My brother knows the head of the Land Bureau," Wang Jianli boasted one day. He was swigging a beer. His white T-shirt was rolled up to his chest as he tried to stay cool. "He told me this whole area will be torn down soon."

"Really? Then we should haggle!" Wang's friend said. "I won't move unless I get a good deal. I want a new apartment at least twice as big. Let's see who can hold out longer, me or the government."

"It's definitely happening. I hear a businessman wants to build a factory here," said another neighbor.

"No way!" Wang Jianli said. "The government is going to build a highway right through this town!"

These discussions went on for hours, covering everything from the size of their future apartments, to the long dining tables, colorful vases, and black leather sofas they would furnish them with. Rushing to the public toilet in their pajamas in the early mornings and clambering up ladders to fix roofs in the rain would be things of the past. I wanted to believe these stories, and not the stories that said we'd be displaced. Instead I, too, thought of what my room would be like. I wouldn't have to share with Yunxiang anymore. I'd put up pretty posters for decoration and read alone in my room. I trusted that the government, as I had been taught, would take care of us. My family and I would be safe.

Villagers thought Lutai townspeople had it made, but only those who lived in the town knew of its difficulties.

People worked as long as twelve hours in the factories, sometimes the whole night if they took the late shift. Those few hours Wang Jianli and his friends spent under the poplar tree could be the happiest moments in their day. For a few hours, they could dream of better jobs and higher earnings. In the town, even locals like the Wangs lived in the cracks, between city and village circumstances. If they hadn't found an "iron rice bowl"—a stable job in a government-backed institution—by now, life in town was almost no better than in the village.

Though the Wangs, Cuis, and other Lutai locals thought they were special, a town is not a city, and they wanted more than anything to become "real city folk." My parents had climbed one step up, from a village to a town, but it was the big race up to the city that every Chinese person wanted to win. Most of us just didn't know how to get there, so it only made the competition more heated. The more migrants could be held back, merely for being outsiders, the fewer people there would be in the race.

Lutai townspeople were not bad. But the country was changing. People like Wang Jianli's parents had felt a sense of security as factory workers in the Mao era, but that security no longer existed. Many migrant workers did what were considered low-level, if necessary, jobs like construction and street cleaning, but when they started entering the factories the Lutai people really began to despise them. Migrants were only supposed to be bike repairmen, trash recyclers, or street vendors—not factory workers. The migrants did any and every kind of work to avoid returning to their villages. Each year, hundreds of thousands of people arrived in big cities like Guangzhou and Beijing, looking for jobs. Even little towns like Lutai could not escape the rising tide. The migrants worked hard and long; they had a greater sense of fear strapped to their backs. Men like Wang Jianli wanted fortune or a life in the city but did nothing to work for it. There were many stories of people quitting their factory jobs and moving to cities like Guangzhou, while Wang complained it was too risky. Once you have stability in China, you don't want to risk it—perhaps you might never have it again. And it took a lot of hard work to keep climbing—there were always people ready to pull you down, especially when you're a migrant.

I learned that one of the worst things to be in China was to be an outsider or different. On the other hand, Wang Jianli's pride at being a local outweighed his desire to work harder and achieve more; he was complacent. My family and I had no such pride of place, and so achievement was all that mattered.

Every day, Wang Jianli longed for the government's demolition order and the fat compensation check it would bring. But the rumors came and went, and Wang Jianli's demolition dreams didn't come true until twenty years later.

CHAPTER FIVE

The Young Patriot

My mother and father began to successfully run the kindergarten. Enrollments increased, but it was my mom's personal mission to use the day care to help migrant families. Some local parents banned their children from playing and studying in the same classroom as migrant children. Most private kindergartens did not want to risk upsetting the local parents, who had more money and were more likely to pay their fees on time. Nor did they tend to be late picking up their children like the migrant parents, who often worked exhaustingly long hours doing manual labor. Such prejudice was only a shadow of the cruelty migrants experienced, and an illustration of how systems are set up to make it tougher for generation after generation to climb out of the cycle of poverty.

Mom made it a priority to help them. Four days a week, I had dinner with other migrant children, who often showed up with dirt-smeared faces or the same juice-stained T-shirt from the day before. Sometimes their parents would not arrive until after 8 p.m., apologizing with sheepish smiles on their worn faces. My mother did not scold them. She knew they were working, and I loved having more friends and tried to help my parents by sharing my toys and creating games for us all to play.

One of my best friends was a girl named Haolin, from Inner Mongolia. Her parents had a roadside car repair shop and worked from seven in the morning to late at night, seven days a week. Sometimes Haolin's mother left her with us on the weekends, and when we visited my grandparents in Caiyuan, we would take her with us.

Though my parents ran a kindergarten and were helping migrant families, we were migrants, too, and faced the same scrutiny. When Yunxiang was ready to start middle school and I primary school, my parents struggled to find places for us. My mom's friend Xiangju asked the headmaster of the school where she taught if we could attend, but the headmaster refused on the basis of our rural *hukou*. The government had issued a regulation saying that children of migrants could go to the local school only if their parents paid extra money. To enroll Yunxiang my parent would have to pay 3,000 yuan for the three-year middle school, and 3,600 yuan for my six-year primary school. In total, it was one quarter of the money my parents had paid for our house. The extra charge was levied because we were "borrowing education resources" from local children. Xiangju advised Mom to give the headmaster "gifts" if we wanted a chance at a school interview.

My parents had so little money. But what would be the point of moving to town and then failing to give us an education? My mother confided in Yunxiang and me. Many migrant families found themselves at this crossroad. They had to either put their children in private schools or send them back home to attend in their village. Yunxiang and I knew bribery was wrong, but we also wanted to attend school. We were all in it together.

A few weeks later, my parents stacked heavy bags of rice on their bicycle seats and placed large, trussed-up crabs— a seasonal specialty—in their baskets for the headmaster. The crabs were each bigger than a rice bowl. I remember my mother's misty eyes as she packed the bags and put some cash in a lucky red envelope. The night before, she had counted out the crisp bills. It was 1,000 yuan, almost two months' living expenses.

Xiangju led my parents to Headmaster Zhang's apartment, which was in one of the nicest compounds in Lutai. Two guards sat in a little house at the entrance and took down their information before letting them in.

Headmaster Zhang looked at my parents as if perplexed, and feigned refusal of the "gifts"...before finally accepting them. When my parents were about to turn to exit, he said, "Children from villages sometimes find it difficult to catch up with Lutai students." My father wanted to argue that his children were smart, but my mother stopped him: *Just smile and nod.*

With the "gifts" and 6,600-yuan extra "fee," Yunxiang and I were accepted. My parents began working harder than ever to maintain our living expenses and school fees. If getting out of the village was a long, hard journey, we were right on track.

*   *   *

I started at Lutai No. 2 Primary School along with Li Chun, whose father had paid a 6,000 yuan extra fee to enroll him, thus gaining him entrance but still not overcoming the fact of his exclusion from taking the *gaokao*, the college entrance exam. The *gaokao* was more competitive in Hunan than in Tianjin or Beijing, where there were fewer students and more quality universities. But the Li family was happy for now. We were both in Xiangju's class.

Everything about school life was new. I set off at 7 a.m., when only street peddlers were about with their carts piled high with apples, cabbage, and shrimp. Carts selling breakfast goodies grew more frequent the closer I got to school. People in the township were too busy to eat the morning meal at home. Misty clouds rose from bamboo steamers smelling of dumplings, and cooks ladled batter onto griddles to make savory pancakes.

At school, a big red welcome banner decorated the gate. Two older students guarded the entrance, standing erect and wearing red sashes across their chests. Whenever a teacher approached the building, they would snap a salute, right hands raised high above their heads, and shout, "Good morning, Teacher!" As the days went along, I noticed they were also placed there to enforce rules. Whenever they noticed a student who was not wearing a name badge, or a student who was not wearing the red neckerchief, they would stop them and note down their name. The teacher in charge of that student's class would get a deduction from their yearly bonus. Xiangju always became furious when any student from her class broke the rules. She would call the student's parents and have the child sent home. The parents would bring Xiangju gifts, a basket of fruit or coupons that could be used at the supermarkets to make up for it. They didn't want the teacher to dislike and fail their child.

One day I forgot to wear my red neckerchief, but as Mom's best friend, Xiangju didn't call; she came to our house after school.

"I had so much trust in Chaoqun, and thought she would be the last one to disappoint me," Xiangju complained. "I've told the headmaster so many good things about her, saying that although Chaoqun is from the village, she can be as good as the Lutai kids... But today I was deeply sorry."

"It's my fault; I should have checked everything before she left home," my mom said with a strained smile. I knew she was furious with me.

I hated to see Mom apologizing for things that weren't her fault. Although Xiangju had been helpful to us, I was fed up with her arrogant attitude, as if she were a god and we should be forever thankful to her. To avoid making the same mistake again, I purchased an extra neckerchief and kept it in my schoolbag.

The school was a collection of low buildings, similar to our *hutong*. Around 750 students from ages seven to thirteen were distributed among eighteen classrooms for six grades.

Our classroom was by an old willow tree in the corner of the schoolyard. Inside about forty students took their seats at tightly packed rows of wooden desks. The blackboard at the back of the room had been decorated with drawings of flowers and animals. This was where announcements would be posted and model students praised.

Four big, bold characters had been written above the front blackboard: *civilized, united, industrious,* and *progressive*. Xiangju said it was the school motto. The national flag—five yellow stars on a red background—was displayed between the characters. On the first day, our assignment was to memorize the motto. We were told we'd soon be tested on all the things we learned about our school and country.

"You see the five stars of the national flag?" she asked.

"Yeeeesss!" we said in unison. We were instructed to answer together, no matter what the question. The trick was to drag the word out for as long as possible. The teachers encouraged it. They liked our answers to be clear and unified, almost military-like. When we had to read out loud, Xiangju would count us in: "One, two, three, start!" If our reading became disjointed, she would make us begin again and again and again until we ended sharply together.

"The big star is the Communist Party, and the four small ones represent the people of all fifty-six ethnic groups, as well as the four social classes. One edge of each small star faces toward the big star. This means the people of all fifty-six groups are united under the leadership of our Communist Party. Understand?" Xiangju asked, looking at us expectantly.

"Underrr...stooood..."

Portraits of famous politicians, scientists, artists, and scholars were placed around the classroom, each with their own quotation:

> There is no such thing as a genius. I spend the time other people spend drinking coffee, writing.
> —Lu Xun, writer and essayist

> Study for a prosperous and rising China.
> —Zhou Enlai, the first premier of the People's Republic of China

Xiangju told us to learn from these famous men, to bear responsibility and to make a contribution to our country. Reciting these quotes was just the first of hundreds of sayings I had to memorize throughout my education. Flags, patriotic quotations, male portraits, and mottos adorned the walls of every classroom I saw until college.

Xiangju also made us memorize the pupil's principles: twenty clauses of dos and don'ts and regulations. We had to repeat them one line at a time:

Love the country, love the people, and love the Chinese Communist Party. Study hard and make progress every day...

"Love the country, love the people, and love the Chinese Communist Party..." We tried to keep up, but the lines were too long for us to remember in one go, as we had no idea what it all meant. We had only the vaguest notion of who "the people" were. The principles might as well have been written by aliens. Even Chinese characters were still a mystery to us.

Xiangju shortened the sentences. "Repeat after me: 'Love the country...'"

Xiangju was known for being strict but competent. All the students were afraid of her, including me. She had big eyes and a powerful voice; three seconds of her gaze could make you quake, and her deep, thunderous voice always echoed. I never told my classmates that Xiangju was a close family friend whom I called Aunt. I did not want them to think I was special or set myself apart in any way. The school encouraged students to work diligently and in synchrony. In addition to reading in one voice, we'd do our morning warm-up exercises to recorded counting broadcast over the loudspeakers. We stood in six lines—three for boys and three for girls—stretched our legs and arms, shook our heads and moved our shoulders, and jumped. A team of students from higher grades inspected us and wrote down a score for each class in a notebook. To earn a higher score, the students had to lift their arms and legs to almost the same height. Again, the score was related to our teacher's annual bonus.

Every morning, we would do eye exercises to music. Following instructions from a poster on the wall, we had to close our eyes and massage acupuncture points around our eye sockets to protect our eyes from disease. Teachers kept close watch in case any of us opened our eyes during the exercise. Cheaters got a lash with the cane on their shoulder, back, arms, or even on their head.

★　★　★

Collectivism has a long history in China. Historically and in accordance with the ideology set out by the great Chinese philosopher, Confucius (551 to 479 BC), the country's interests are more important than a family's, and the interests of a family should be put ahead of the individual's. Confucians believe that, if necessary, one should restrain his personal desire to achieve the goals of benevolence and righteousness in the society. Such ideas were encouraged by feudal dynasties, which in turn helped the feudal rulers to consolidate governing. When Confucius's doctrine worked, people tended to think collectively for the greater good, and to obey the empire's rulings without disturbance.

The Chinese Communist Party adopted collectivization from the Soviet Union. Although it crushed most other traditional Chinese ideologies in its first thirty years of ruling, collectivist ideology happened to be useful, and was tolerated and even encouraged. Individualism was equated to bourgeois liberalization—the opposite of Mao's goal. In Communist China, people were made to be proud of sacrificing their personal interests for the good of a unified nation.

Though China made progress in its various industries—including defense, mining, railway, and manufacturing, it ignored the needs of its citizens for such things as food, clothes, and individual freedom. The emphasis on collectivism led to many tragedies, and the notion of overtaking the West led to ultra-leftist ideas. The goals were too ambitious and too broad, and most of the time were impractical. In addition, to criticize or challenge the "shared goal" was regarded as reactionary and just about treasonous.

With the launch of Reform and Opening Up in 1978, China began to allow not only private enterprise but also sought foreign investment and engagement with the West. Yet despite early successes, some party leaders believed the policy helped cause a lack of belief in socialism and Marxism, and distrust of the party in general, as well as a noticeable economic divide between rich and poor. This crisis peaked in the late 1980s when officials—from the top of government to the village chiefs—began more openly taking bribes and also to embezzle funds. For example, while the children of government officials had power and plenty of resources for their future, college graduates who had no connections could not find jobs.

In the spring of 1989—the year I was born—people, mostly young college students, protested peacefully in Beijing's Tiananmen Square and other big cities, calling for freedom of the press and government accountability, among other goals. They wanted a degree of democratic reforms.

On June 4, fifty days after the protests had begun, the government sent in the army and their tanks to quell the demonstrations—in a confrontation that soon became violent with the military, who were armed, overwhelming the square. Several hundred to more than two thousand people, mostly students, were killed. The exact number is unknown; the authorities have never given a full account of the casualties, and the unwritten rule—in one of the most glaring examples of self-censorship—forbids anyone from talking about it, much less writing about it, in an attempt to sweep away its memory. Though in places like Hong Kong and Taiwan, memorial services and public vigils are held every year on the June Fourth anniversary.

The party attributed the breakout of the protest to the lack of "education," or belief in a proper Communist ideology. The younger generation, who by then had been influenced by Western literature, music, and film, had begun talking about democracy and freedom. As a result, the party launched a patriotic-education campaign in schools and colleges that continues to this day with the aim of re-establishing political beliefs and loyalty to the Communist state. Many of my schoolbooks were full of articles about loving the country and admiring the party. In an almost brainwashing method, they made me believe if I was not a patriot and party lover, then I was committing the most serious crime.

Our "education" was delivered in history, political science, and even Chinese-language classes, where I was constantly told to be loyal, that only the party could make Chinese people's lives better and protect China from the threats of hostile countries like Japan and America. In addition to celebrating China's history and traditions, we were told there was still work to be done but that we had overcome our shortcomings against the West; China mustn't be disturbed by Western-style democracy, which would destabilize our society—all this was taught to me in primary school. Our "education" was indoctrinated into our mentalities and to question it was wrong and, even more, unacceptable.

*　　*　　*

Every Monday, we held a flag-raising ceremony where we sang the national anthem. It was the most important part of the week. Chatting was forbidden, and we were instructed to look serious. Volunteers from the upper grades noted down the class and name of any student caught talking or laughing, as well as those whose uniforms were not up to par. I stood straight and looked at the flag with as much honor as I could muster. Xiangju said if I behaved well, she would recommend me to hold the flag the following year. My parents would be proud of me. I was eager to prove to my teacher that, although I was from a village, I could be one of the best students in the class.

From my very first day, I was repeatedly told how glorious it was to be a Young Pioneer, although nearly every six- to fourteen-year-old in China was a member. We had to wear our red neckerchief religiously. The Young Pioneers' prestige came from its affiliation with the Communist Youth League, an organization of students from middle school to university that operated directly under the Communist Party of China and which was a training ground for future party leaders. We were told the neckerchief was red because it was stained by the blood of revolutionary martyrs who sacrificed their lives for China's bright future. We wore it out of respect for them and to demonstrate how much we appreciated the good life we lived as a result of their selfless acts of courage.

Our first ever history lesson was about the Opium War in 1840 and the victory of the War of Resistance against Japan in 1945. The lessons were meant to unify us, by pointing at a shared enemy for all—mainly the British, Japanese, and Americans. As a young student, I was made to understand that British people were bad long, long ago, because they stole everything that belonged to us, from prized treasures and relics looted from the Summer Palace or territories seized from us—like Hong Kong, which when handed back to China in 1997 was cause for great celebration.

I thought Americans were just strange. From what I saw and heard, they were a walking contradiction, nice but evil, romantic but cruel. I was confused. I watched films like *Forrest Gump* and *Titanic*, where everyone seemed nice—from Tom Hanks saving Lieutenant Dan in Vietnam to Leonardo DiCaprio saving the love of his life. We couldn't get enough of these films—pirated DVDs were cheap and available in every market—or the American actors, but then our political science teacher would say things like, "The Americans' plan is to beat us and make a mess of our country."

In my mind, the Japanese were pure evil, and should never be removed from the blacklist, because they killed so many Chinese people in the war and still deny it, as I was told.

★   ★   ★

After Grandfather Wengui died, we visited Chaoyang to see Nainai and my other grandparents in Caiyuan Village once a month. I considered it paradise outside my new life in town. I found, though, that while Lutai was changing, and changing me, so were the villages. Uncle Lishui and a few neighbors even had a telephone installed in their homes. In Caiyuan, people wanted larger houses, so they filled in the ponds with earth and silt, and built houses over them. I was sad to see the water gone, the areas I had picked lilies and lotus flowers.

While some things had changed, other things remained stuck between the past and the future. Families still cooked on stoves heated with fires made of wood and straw, but they also had a tin of natural gas in their kitchens for special occasions.

Seeing my mother's loving parents, my grandpa (Laoye) and grandma (Laolao), and my cousins always brought a smile to my face. Chunting was fascinated by my stories about Lutai, and I'm ashamed to admit her curiosity made me feel superior. I never told her about how inferior we were treated in the *hutong*. I liked being the hero when we returned to the village. While we had music, art, and English classes in the fourth grade, Chunting's school only had Chinese and math. We had smart, sailor-like school uniforms; they had none. She did not get to go on trips to the cinema, as we did. When I spoke to Chunting about my life, I felt good about myself.

I told her about how on the way to the cinema we always stood in two long lines, wearing identical yellow hats and walking hand in hand when crossing the road at traffic lights. I enthusiastically described the films I had watched.

The movies about the war between China and Japan (1937 to 1945) look great on the big screen. I bragged, "Not like on TV. Our soldiers look awesome fighting the Japanese!" I liked to exaggerate how good the films were because I enjoyed the excited and envious looks on her and my other cousins' faces.

We went on school trips to the cinema three or four times a semester, but half of the films were about China's war with Japan or the civil war between the Communist party and the Chinese Nationalists, the Kuomintang, who lost the war and fled to Taiwan. Actually I felt bored when I watched those films, and was always confused by the plot, which always ended more or less the same, with the Chinese triumphant. Also, I had never met a Kuomintang member in my life. The Japanese and the Kuomintang soldiers were always the bad guys in the films, and the Communist Party soldiers were heroes. After all, they'd built an independent country for the Chinese people and led them toward a bright future.

It was almost as if the directors had read our textbooks as well.

I told Chunting how the teachers made us write "reviews" when we returned from the cinema. "I always write: 'I should learn from the heroes to be fearless and to die for our country,'" I said, reciting a sentence I had memorized from a collection of essays.

"Is that what you really think?" Chunting asked, her eyes bright with intrigue.

"No!" I snapped. "Do you write what you actually think in your school essays? My teachers say that what matters is getting the answer right, not your opinions!"

I wasn't joking. In our exams, the standard for answering correctly was always the same. The best answers conveyed patriotism, selflessness, devotion, and grand dreams for the nation: for example, the desire to become an astronaut to bring great honor to China.

Many of my weekends were spent with Chunting and

our friends in Laoye's house. Chunting and I would sit on wooden stools; our friends on the floor. I told them that on Tomb Sweeping Day in April, we made white paper flowers to attach to the chest pockets of our school uniforms and marched to the Martyrs' Cemetery. In front of the heroes' tombs, we had to keep silent for three minutes before walking beside the gravestones, throwing our flowers onto them.

I told them about Children's Day, when we had a big ceremony for the students from my class who had become Communist Young Pioneers. The teachers put red scarves around our shoulders, and we vowed to be prepared to sacrifice ourselves for the mission of Communism.

Chunting looked especially envious when I told that story. She was a Young Pioneer, too, but her school did nothing to mark the big day.

I told them how on the days before the officials from the Tianjin Education Bureau came to our school for inspection, we were busy cleaning our classrooms and campus, and students whose uniforms were not clean on inspection day were sent home until the officials left.

Listening to these stories, my village friends always giggled and begged for more. Their favorite one was about how we were forced to cry together while watching the funeral of Deng Xiaoping, China's paramount leader.

On that day Dean Li, the school administrator, arrived with three tall boys from the upper grades, carrying a television. My classmates became excited and started cheering. A girl followed them in, carrying a picture of an old man that she hung on the blackboard. Dean Li whispered something to Xiangju. They looked stern, not sharing a smile as they usually did.

"Dear students." Xiangju turned to address us while Dean Li walked to the back of the classroom. "Did you know, our dear grandpa Deng Xiaoping has passed away?" She paused, screwing up her face into a grimace.

"I know you are so sad, as am I," she continued. "Thanks to our headmaster's support, we can all watch the funeral and pay our respects to Grandpa Deng together. You can cry."

Cry? I could not believe what I was hearing. Since our first day, we had always been scolded for crying in school. Now we could cry together? For this old man?

"Stand up and pay silent tribute to Grandpa Deng!" Xiangju ordered.

I stood up, stifling a laugh. I didn't even know who Deng Xiaoping was. The old man in the photo was smiling. I looked around at my classmates, wondering if any of them knew. They looked just as confused.

"I know you want to weep for our dearest grandpa Deng," Xiangju said.

"Who's Grandpa Deng?" I asked.

Xiangju threw me a razor-sharp look.

"Deng Xiaoping is known as the architect of China's Reform and Opening Up," Dean Li said. "He is much admired for his determination in the negotiations with the UK to return Hong Kong to us. It is so sad he couldn't live to see the handover ceremony." China and the UK had planned to hold the ceremony that coming July, a few months after Deng died.

We all wanted to be good students and please Xiangju, who obviously wanted us to weep. I saw some of my classmates trying, but clearly struggling.

Xiangju and Li walked around, peering attentively at our faces, and though a few good students managed to squeeze out a tear, a couple of others burst out laughing and were immediately sent out of the room.

I didn't understand how I could cry for somebody I didn't know.

Mom told me the story of how hard she and her friends cried when the death of Chairman Mao was announced in 1976, and how it felt like the end of the world. Did they want us to cry like that? Her generation worshipped Mao when they were young, but my generation no longer fanatically admired any politician, not even Deng Xiaoping.

*   *   *

Most Chinese people might not be politically active, but many are politically chatty. A Beijing cabbie could analyze happenings in government more vividly than any political science professor.

"A US fighter jet bombed the Chinese embassy in Belgrade!" Wang Jianli shouted between swigs of his *baijiu*, the popular rice liquor. "Damn the Americans!"

His voice, together with the sounds of bottles clanking to the ground, startled me out of my nap. I stuck my head out the window. He had one hand on his hip, and his eyes were red with anger. Glass fragments from broken beer bottles were scattered on the ground around him. He was talking about the bombing in Yugoslavia, which happened early that morning. It wasn't until 7 p.m. that most people learned about it. *Xinwen Lianbo*, China Central Television (CCTV) network's most popular daily news broadcast, covered it.

In the spring of 1999, the US-led NATO troops decided to attack Yugoslavia to stop its president, Slobodan Miloše-vić, from encouraging marginalized Serbs to attack the Kosovar Albanians, who had formed a separatist movement. On the morning of May 8, 1999 (Beijing time), NATO bombed the Chinese embassy in Belgrade, Serbia (a republic of Yugoslavia before it broke up into various countries including Bosnia, Croatia, Herzegovina, Macedonia, Kosovo, and Slovenia), killing three Chinese journalists. American officials insisted it was a mistake, but Chinese officials accused the US of a deliberate attack, and so did Chinese citizens, who also believed the bombing was an intentional assault on our country.

"It's a message!" Wang shouted. "Americans are telling the Chinese, 'From now on, don't make a fuss about what we do, otherwise we'll teach you a lesson.'"

They all spat out curses against the Americans.

"Officials today don't have guts like Mao Zedong did!" another old man said. "They're cowards! If Mao were alive today, we wouldn't have to be afraid of stupid American threats!"

A younger man who worked in our local government office also joined in. "We're still too weak. Americans have aircraft carriers and can send people to space; what can we do? 'Weak countries don't have diplomacy,' as the saying goes. We should keep quiet and focus on industry."

I was fascinated, because I had never heard people criticize our government and the Communist Party in this way! When I told my mom what they were saying, she said such talk would have landed them in prison during her time. I was afraid, but to hear this conversation was like eating vanilla ice cream all my life and then tasting chocolate for the first time. I couldn't resist listening.

That week was pure chaos. My school ordered the students to write an essay about the incident. The news anchors condemned the violence led by NATO and the US, and the village of one of the journalists killed was renamed in his honor as "Xinghu" Village. Angry students wearing T-shirts and holding flags with anti-American slogans gathered at the US embassy. In Lutai, anti-American posters were plastered outside schools, shopping malls, post offices, and hospitals, with messages like "CHINESE PEOPLE ARE ANGRY THIS TIME." Police and protestors seemed to be everywhere.

In third grade, my classmates and I were too young to go to any protest, but on the first Monday after the bombing, my school organized all the students to assemble outside in the playground in front of the national flag, which was at half-mast. Headmaster Zhang read out a script he had prepared, denouncing the US as evil. "Dear students, remember this day. Work hard and be strong. Only when we are strong enough will the outlaw countries respect us."

It felt like a sacred moment. I looked at the red neckerchief I was wearing and thought about what he had said.

Chinese officials and my parents and teachers seemed to always talk as if China was bullied and had to protect itself. *The American government is bad, and we should trust that the Communist Party will make China strong.* Why were they bad? Was it just because of one bombing? But the teachers had been saying that about Americans since I was in kindergarten. We had been taught this our entire lives. Nobody bothered to explain why. Maybe because we were too young. But then, why were we old enough to hate foreign countries and their people?

I didn't know what to write about the bombing. The news and events left me confused. Should my essay be full of hatred? I had only just learned how to say bad things about Japan, which had been the forever enemy in our grandparents' and parents' conversations, and the anti-Japan narrative had dominated our curriculum. Of course, I had read essays about the bad behavior of the US, but it was hard for me to sit down and write of my own contempt for a country I knew little about and had never visited.

My friends and I actually liked American things. I dreamed of one day going to Disneyland to meet Mickey Mouse. Yunxiang was crazy about Nike shoes. Li Chun loved Superman so much that he covered everything he used at school—his pencil box, books, and rulers—with the images of the strong white American hero. Even Headmaster Zhang proudly bragged about a watch he wore that was purchased in America. He was the only person I knew who had been to the US, and I overheard that he liked it. However, Headmaster Zhang would say things like the

American government was evil but the American people were good. That was even more confusing.

What happened to the good people once they started jobs in the government? I thought.

But it did not matter whether things made sense to me or not—in the classroom, we had to say bad things about America.

I spent all evening sitting at my desk writing—then crossing out sentences. *It won't end well for the ugly American politicians with their evil policy toward China*, I wrote. But I thought Americans were not so ugly looking, and besides, I had no idea what "politicians" were and what "policy" really meant.

The Chinese Communist Party and the people won't let troublemaking America realize their conspiracy. No, again. What was the conspiracy? I could not find the right words. What did the party have to do with my feelings? Of course I was angry at the US soldiers who had killed the Chinese journalists, but I could not make myself hate them. I had never even met an American!

Desperate, I turned to my parents. My father had acquired a rich collection of quotes, thanks to his involvement in political movements during his youth. He let me sit on his lap and recited funny sentences for me to write down. From his suggestions, I chose: *Imperialism will never abandon its intention to destroy us!* and *All reactionaries are just paper tigers!* They sounded like something Xiangju wanted to hear, but they did not mean anything to me. Baba said they were famous quotes by Chairman Mao, and that Mao had been good at making up sentences that sounded weird or didn't make sense. There was even a little red book of his strange quotes. In this way, I managed to finish my task.

Soon after, the street banners were gone, and *Xinwen Lianbo* reported less and less on the bombing until one day their anchors were allowed to smile. And Wang and his friends started to complain about CCTV, wondering when they would start broadcasting NBA games again.

CHAPTER SIX

The Gods vs. the Ghosts

China's *qigong* (pronounced chi-gong) boom began in the 1980s, a time when people were beginning to explore different forms of exercise, meditation, and spirituality. And soon after Falun Gong was founded in 1992, it became the most popular one. Within months, about a hundred villagers in Caiyuan, one-tenth of the population, had begun to follow Falun Gong, including my grandfather Laoye.

"It's nonsense!" Uncle Shoukui complained over the phone to Mom. "Dad is practicing that? He's a party member and should. believe in Marxism—not God, heaven, or ghosts." Uncle Shoukui had recently been appointed senior attorney in the Lutai Town Judicial Bureau. He firmly believed in party ideology and could hardly believe that his father, who had been the first party member in the village and so an atheist by default, had "succumbed."

My mother knew he would be upset, but understood that Laoye was not the only one who was practicing the "superstition," as it was called.

Falun Gong (or Falun Dafa), founded by Li Hongzhi, is a form of Buddhist qigong—the practice of cultivating life force, or qi, through a set of physical movements, breathing exercises, and meditation techniques. It is based on a philosophy of truthfulness, compassion, and forbearance. It also claims to incorporate elements of Taoism, a religious and philosophical tradition that emphasizes living in harmony with everything. The villagers believed that with good morals and regular meditation, they could free themselves of attachments to the physical world and ultimately achieve spiritual enlightenment. And perhaps more importantly, it made villagers of my grandfather's generation feel as if they belonged to a movement again, for the first time in a long while.

"Li Hongzhi is a messenger sent by Sakyamuni, the founder of Buddhism," Laoye told me when I was visiting him one weekend. "He created Falun Gong to save the people and take them to heaven when the world ends, which will happen soon." His eyes sparkled as he spoke. He pointed to a portrait hanging on his bedroom wall of Li Hongzhi next to the portrait of Chairman Mao.

Our science teachers had told us that all religions were superstitions. At the age of ten, I had no clue what religion really was. I didn't believe in any god, angels, fairies, spirits, or ghosts. At school, we were taught to be atheists, no exception. If a student said they believed in God, the other students would isolate him and label him a lunatic. We had no discussion about what spiritual beliefs were and what they could bring to people. As was the case with many other topics, as students, we were told to conclude only that religion pollutes people's minds by making them care less about their current life. That was that.

I was convinced that only uncivilized people, who probably never went to school, believed in such things.

But Laoye has read a lot of books. How could he fall for it? I also wondered.

As I listened to Mom on the phone with Uncle, I went into Laoye's room to examine the portrait of Li Hongzhi. Master Li, as practitioners called him, was sitting cross-legged on a lotus-shaped cushion. His eyes were closed and his hands rested in front of him, his upturned palms resting on top of each other. He looked calm. Golden halos crowned his head, just as they crowned Buddha's in the books and movies I saw. They symbolized Master Li's magnificent energy and power. The villagers had never seen a computer or heard of Photoshop, so it looked real to them.

It was Cripple Feng who brought Falun Gong to the village and sold the doctored pictures of Li for five yuan a piece.

Cripple Feng had polio as a child and was left with a lame left leg, which earned her the nickname. In her fifties, she learned of Falun Gong during a trip to see her cousin in a neighboring village. Her cousin, who had been practicing for years, told Feng how believers never became ill, thanks to their devotion to Master Li and his teachings. If Cripple Feng followed Master Li, even her leg would one day be healed, her cousin said. It sounded ridiculous to me, like something from science fiction. But at the same time,

I wished the miracle would really happen so I could see it. If Cripple Feng were no longer crippled, I wondered, then what would we call her?

Cripple Feng was converted when she attended a gathering her cousin had organized at home. Feng was touched by the scene of dozens of people sitting in the same room, chanting: "Falun Dafa is good." It reminded her of the time during the Cultural Revolution when all the Red Guards chanted, "Long live Chairman Mao!" Feng had been a Red Guard, too, and liked the feeling of unity. By the third night, she was no longer just Cripple Feng; she was a believer.

When she returned to Caiyuan the next day, she announced her new identity and told the story of her conversion. It was the first time anyone in the village had openly admitted to spiritual belief since the Cultural Revolution, over thirty years before.

As a devout believer, Feng turned the largest room of her farmhouse into the Falun Gong Practicing Center. Lotus-shaped cushions, Falun Gong books, and DVDs featuring Li giving speeches arrived by the van load outside her front door. Feng resold everything to the villagers, making a tidy profit. Some questioned her motives, whispering that her devotion to Master Li was just a scam. But the doubt disappeared when Feng began hosting free DVD screenings and discussion groups every evening.

Perplexed by Laoye's devotion, Uncle Shoukui quizzed my grandfather on his belief, but Laoye argued that it was a good thing, teaching people to be kind and helping those in pain to suffer less, which was in sync with his beliefs, not separate from them.

"Then what about Chairman Mao? Are you still an atheist?" Uncle Shoukui asked. "Both your idols will be furious, I'm afraid."

"I'm almost eighty," Laoye replied patiently. "At my age, such things do not matter as much as they used to. It's not all black and white."

To me, Laoye's response made sense; it went along with how I felt about Chinese politics and Disneyland.

Reading Li Hongzhi's books and practicing tai chi–style exercises became an important part of Laoye's daily life. Chunting and I would imitate Laoye's movements, sending ourselves into fits of giggles while he moved his arms and legs gracefully to the music coming from his tapes. He moved slowly and gently, and he remained expressionless. He knew we were behind him, of course, but he never got angry. If we were especially noisy, he would open his eyes and look back at us, giving us a tolerant smile as we made faces at him before running out into the yard. He'd just close his eyes again and return to his exercise.

If Falun Gong is superstition, then superstition is not all bad, I thought.

Laoye's temper had cooled down and he became much nicer. He no longer chased the street cats with a bamboo stick when they stole his salted fish hanging behind the house. Now he felt all lives were equal and that he didn't have the right to punish others, even the naughty cats. I began to like how superstition had softened his heart. Of course, I dared not tell my parents or uncle that!

Laoye might have been a firm believer, but he drew the

line at attending gatherings. Acutely aware of his party membership, he didn't want people talking.

How should a party member behave? The question perplexed both Laoye and me.

Laoye had been among the first to get up and plow the fields of the People's Commune. When villagers began to starve during the three years of the Great Famine, he worked in the public kitchen, making sure everyone was fed before ladling out his own meager portion. He and his family suffered, but he never doubted the revolution. He was a member of the Communist Party, he'd tell my grandmother, who was often pale from malnutrition. She felt her health should be his first priority, but he would not betray Chairman Mao, believing that a good party member sacrifices for others.

Thirty years later, he felt the new party members were letting people down. They used their authority to grab the best land for themselves, bought the best and newest car models, and lived in the tallest houses—a brazen sign of their wealth. Their behavior confused Laoye.

He did not approve of these new-style party members, but clearly times had changed and Mao's way no longer seemed as compelling. For Laoye, Falun Gong filled a gap, and gave him a renewed sense of purpose and belonging.

My grandmother Laolao, who was also a follower, called her husband a hypocrite. She said he was not completely devoted to Falun Gong because he did not attend the gatherings and did not read all the books. But Laoye ignored her needling. When and where he practiced and what books he read were beside the point: in his heart he believed.

*   *   *

Now that Laoye seemed to have the most tolerance and patience out of all the adults at home, Chunting and I followed him around like two tails. To keep us occupied, he'd tell us stories, especially those about his life. I found his stories to be the most telling. Laoye once had riches, the likes of which his children would never see. He would narrow his eyes and point at a waving green sea of rice on the far side of the river.

"Look," he once told us. "Long ago, before your parents were born—before even the People's Liberation Army liberated this place—all that used to be ours."

"You're lying," I said, standing on a chair to catch ladybugs so I could put them in Laoye's white beard. "If all that was ours, why are you not rich?"

"Sometimes being poor is better than being rich," Laoye laughed. "You're too young to understand."

I learned Laoye's story bit by bit until I could piece together a vague picture of his earlier life.

My grandfather's given name was Yuying, which means "fine as jade." Born into a family who owned many, many *mu* of land and a timber shop, he had a loving mother and wealthy father. However, when my grandfather was twelve years old, his father brought home a concubine, a woman he knew from the local gambling den. Laoye fought with his dad over this for years and finally left the village when he was fourteen to work in a silk shop in a city called Jinzhou. After three years of apprenticeship, Laoye returned, to be greeted by the news that his mother had poisoned herself a few weeks after he left. His father knew Laoye would be angry and banned other family members from sending a letter to inform him of her death.

Laoye's hatred of his father grew.

His father wore the finest clothes and hats in the village and never touched crops or soil.

Laoye was growing inspired by Chairman Mao's revolutionary theories. China needed to create a better future for the poor; the chairman and the Communists had ideas about how to do it.

By the time the Communists marched into Caiyuan Village, Laoye's father had lost everything to gambling debts apart from a house for each of his four sons. The gamblers to whom he had lost his land were later beaten to death when the Communist Party launched land reforms and encouraged the attack of "local tyrants."

Laoye joined the army in the 1940s. It was after two years of fighting in the civil war against the Kuomintang that he became one of the first Communist Party members in the village. At first, he considered it a great honor, but his zeal soon faded. Being a party member meant being a pioneer and leader who served the people and made sacrifices for his country, but soon the way the party ruled began to grate on him.

Laoye began to wonder if he was a pure proletarian revolutionary—the ideal espoused by Chairman Mao. He was too fond, in my grandmother's words, of "impractical" things. He sang Peking opera as he farmed, hung beautiful ink drawings on his wall, and spent evenings sitting in a bamboo chair, listening to the radio. He wrote calligraphy couplets and built nests for swallows under his roof. He lit incense in the temple and prayed. Such interests were—during the revolution—considered to be dangerously bourgeois eccentricities. His duty, as a patriot, was to set an example for others, so my dedicated Laoye decided to remove the Buddhist shrine from his desk and take down the image of the goddess Guanyin. In their place, he put up portraits of Chairman Mao and other party leaders.

The Communist Party had drawn clean lines for religious groups. At a meeting with China's Christian representatives in 1950, Premier Zhou Enlai declared that although religion was a form of idealism—different from the materialism the Communists believed in—the party would "not launch campaigns against religion" and promised to "not carry out Marxist propaganda work in the Catholic churches." But he also said: "We hope our friends from religious circles will not carry out missionary work in the street." In addition, the party founded organizations to scrutinize religions—Buddhism, Taoism, Islam, Catholicism, and Protestantism—and manage their development.

Of course, the nonintervention promise did not last. In 1957, Mao began to fear that portions of the party were moving toward being "soft Communists." Religious leaders became targets and enemies of the people. Religion itself was devalued as a superstition, a sign of backwardness. Eventually, religion was banned altogether in 1966, at the start of the Cultural Revolution, categorized alongside traditional Chinese culture, art, and philosophy as evil. The revolutionaries had their own ideas about culture that they believed to be progressive, and the Red Guards set about dispelling monks, destroying temples, smashing idols, and burning countless, often priceless, religious texts.

Laoye thought the Red Guards were going too far. Buddhism and Taoism had been part of Chinese culture for centuries. Faith gave the poor comfort and hope. Why should it be banned, and people punished for believing?

But faithful Laoye told himself his own doubt was a flaw, or that he must not be smart enough to understand Mao's plan. The chairman had overcome so many difficulties—leading the party to victory against all odds—there must be reasons unseen by the common people why religion was not tolerated. To Grandfather, his mind was the one that needed fixing, not Mao's.

*   *   *

In the early 1980s, China rehabilitated the religious scholars and practitioners attacked during the Cultural Revolution, reopened temples and mosques, and decreased its vigilance against religious activities.

People quickly flocked back to organized religion and spirituality. Mao had been not only a dictator, but also a god of a kind of religion and they were hungry for something to take his place—to fill the vacuum left by his death. This included Falun Gong, created in northeast China in 1992 by Li Hongzhi, who eventually gathered 70 to 100 million practitioners, from farmers and steel workers to students and university professors.

The faith spread by word of mouth and pamphlets.

"Your father is rereading every book he has ever read," Laolao complained to my mom one day during one of our visits. "What a strange old man he is turning into." She spoke quietly, covering her mouth with one hand, even though Laoye's hearing was very bad. I knew this because while his Peking opera was on, I had to clear my throat and speak so loudly for him to hear me.

"So what's wrong with him?" my mom asked, turning her head to be sure Laoye wasn't listening. "He's suddenly become an old man. Sometimes he acts so weird."

"He's afraid of death," Laolao said. "Three friends of his died last winter. When your father heard the funeral music, he just sat home. I asked him why he didn't go to pay his respects but he didn't answer me. They were his childhood friends. I'm worried that he's running from death."

I was too young to understand life and death, but I knew Mom and my grandmother didn't get Laoye. Being immortal was not what he wanted. It was the opposite of their thinking. Li Hongzhi promised him a peaceful transit from this life to the next, as well as a place where he would see the people he used to know and love. Communism and atheism didn't.

★   ★   ★

On another visit to my grandparents, my mom's cousin Kuoxiang came by to give us the latest transcript of Master Li's speech.

"I don't get a cold or even a cough these days." Kuoxiang held Mom's hands and looked into her eyes. "That is a blessing from the practice." She was so focused on Mom that she seemed to not see me standing beside them.

Kuoxiang did look healthier. But it could have been a result of quitting smoking, as Falun Gong required. She looked younger, too, because she had also cut her hair short, according to the belief that hair is the sign of attachment to the troubles in the secular world. She didn't seem to care that this idea was actually from Buddha, not Master Li.

"I'm too busy to practice Falun Gong," Mom said, trying to hide her annoyance. "I have to teach and have two children to take care of." She moved back to the cabbage she was chopping for my lunch. Mom was right; she had no time even for herself. She had to take care of Yunxiang and me and the kindergarten, and spent weekends in the village helping her parents.

"Being busy is not a reason..." Kuoxiang pulled a stool over and sat down. She recounted the stories of the miracles of Falun Gong. "As a child, Master Li Hongzhi once forgot to take his backpack with him to school. He had to return home to get it but didn't have a house key. So he meditated outside, focusing all his energy on the bag, and his soul flew into his house and retrieved it."

I almost burst into laughter. How could she believe such nonsense! I wanted to say something, but Mom looked my way. I once daydreamed about being a kung fu master and flying across the school rooftops to impress my friends, but I knew it was just a fantasy. How could a fortysomething grown-up like Kuoxiang possibly believe that story was true?

She turned to me. "Don't you want to have powers like Master Li, Chaoqun?"

"I would, but my parents want me to spend more time studying," I replied with a small smile.

"Well, if you want to go to a good university, Falun Gong can make you better at school too."

I smiled again. It seemed Kuoxiang had an answer for everything to make Falun Gong sound appealing. That annoyed me.

When Mom and her sister-in-law, my aunt Zhirong, finished cooking and setting the table, Kuoxiang found an excuse to leave. It was impolite to stay for a family's mealtime. After she left, my father, who had been sitting in the living room playing Chinese chess with Zhirong's husband, Uncle Lishui, said, "She must be crazy." He was one of the few people in my family, besides Uncle Shoukui, who was openly against Falun Gong. He felt it was superstitious but also politically dangerous.

"Why?" Mom asked. "People like it simply because it gives them hope. It teaches them to be kind. And for others, like Father, Falun Gong's also a good exercise practice."

"That's right," said Aunt Zhirong. "Politically dangerous? I don't even know how to write my name; how do you expect me to join an uprising?" She burst into laughter.

Baba was easily embarrassed and didn't like the women ganging up against him. When he noticed me sitting at the desk, listening, he shouted, "You go and study! This discussion is not for you. Don't be misled by all this superstitious stuff!"

Uncle Lishui handed some meat from the plate to my father. "Eat! Drink some *baijiu*," he said soothingly.

I looked away so I wouldn't anger Baba, but the truth was

that watching Laoye practice Falun Gong had changed my idea of spirituality. He was still the sensible man he used to be. I didn't understand why Baba said it could be dangerous when it was so calming and helpful to my grandfather. I thought of spirituality or Falun Gong as a hobby—if Laoye and all these people enjoyed doing it, I didn't understand the point in stopping them. If it were a card game, what would be the difference? There were worse things people did with their time. Would it make sense to punish people for those hobbies?

Before long we found Caiyuan was not the only place where I could be "misled." Falun Gong had spread to Lutai. The practitioners, with their long white shirts, were everywhere.

"A tall tree catches the wind first." Baba cited this old proverb to remind Mom of the dangers of Falun Gong. When somebody stands out like a tall tree, he is the most obvious attack target. My father's theory was that the party wouldn't allow so many people to be led by one man for very long.

My mom laughed as if it were a joke. But Dad's theory soon proved to be true.

*   *   *

One summer day in 1999, I was watching cartoons when they were interrupted by an emergency announcement on CCTV: "Falun Gong is an illegal organization and is now banned."

What followed was a long montage of cases where Falun

Gong practitioners either murdered others or committed suicide. The government said Falun Gong was turning people mad and that Li Hongzhi was a fraud.

My father was reading the newspaper in the living room. Upon hearing the news, he called out to my mother, "Cult! We'd better stop your father and brother from being members."

My mother was stunned by what she saw.

Media like CCTV was controlled by the government, and whatever they broadcast was equivalent to an official announcement. Yet people trusted the news. Neither the source nor the truth was questioned.

The next day, street committees posted a notice from the Ministry of Public Security:

The government has decided that Falun Gong is an illegal organization, and now the orders are as follows: no banners, images, emblems, or other signs belonging to Falun Gong are allowed to be displayed in public; the government does not allow anyone to spread books, audio and video products, and other materials related to Falun Gong anywhere...

The notice also banned petitioning and any protest supporting Falun Gong. Another notice came a few days later: people had to hand in their Falun Gong books and any of its products that week. Harboring these products was now a crime. *If you find anybody practicing Falun Gong or using related products at home, please report them to the police,* the notices read.

More notices were posted at my school. During breaks, many of us stood at the information board reading the notices over and over again. I didn't tell my friends that my grandfather and uncle were Falun followers. I noticed that none of the other students admitted to this either. We all just read the announcement as if it did not pertain to the people we loved.

Warnings against Falun Gong increased. At school is where I noticed it most. We watched movies, visited exhibitions, and read articles explaining how evil Falun Gong was. We were told the cult turned people into ruthless killers. In one such documentary, Falun Gong was compared with other cults like America's Peoples Temple and Japan's Aum Shinrikyo. None of us had heard of those cults, but the documentary said many followers of those cults also killed themselves. The films were bloody, with gruesome images of members cutting open their stomachs. Teachers told us stories of how entire families set themselves on fire in pursuit of "heaven." It was instilled in us that Falun Gong would ruin our own families and our future.

One day, when my class was watching one of these anticult documentaries, my classmate Hong stood up and shouted, "Falun Gong is good!"

The entire class gasped, and Teacher Li's face turned crimson.

"I was a practitioner and so were my parents. This stuff you're showing is nonsense!" The entire class stared at her with open mouths. Teacher Li ran over and dragged Hong by her sleeve out of the classroom. The door slammed, and we all just looked at each other in disbelief while the documentary played on. I wondered what would happen to Hong.

Her mother took her home that afternoon, and Hong returned a week later. After the incident, we all kept our distance from her. Everyone worried that she was "abnormal" and that talking to her would turn us crazy like in the films we watched. I didn't believe this would happen and wanted to talk to her but was afraid I might be shunned by my other friends.

To ensure that Chinese people remained loyal to the party, a huge organization like Falun Gong had to be suppressed. The movement's ever-growing members—their ability to organize—made it a threat. This was when my fear of the government began to increase, and I began to shy away from politics instead of embrace it as I'd been taught.

As I now understood it, the government was the only judge of right or wrong. As a Chinese person, my individuality and beliefs did not matter, and I would always lose in any fight with the government.

My generation had more in common with my parents than I thought. It was evident to me that, although our dictator Mao had been dead for decades, China was far from being a free country.

Falun Gong members wrote letters to newspapers and protested outside of government buildings to no avail. The police arrested them for "picking quarrels" and "stirring up trouble," terms that were often used to imprison human rights activists.

Because my parents were not members, the street committee officials never examined our home. However, I spent a lot of time in Caiyuan and saw how the chief enforced the anti–Falun Gong policy on the villagers. Through the loudspeakers on every corner, there were alarming announcements like: *All villagers: Attention, attention. Anybody who practices Falun Gong in public will be jailed. You might be sent to prison and your children will be disqualified from attending college.*

The police drove from village to village to confiscate the Falun materials and publications. Signs like "REFUSE CULTS" were posted next to the One-Child Policy posters.

One day when I was having lunch with my grandparents, Uncle Lishui, Aunt Zhirong, and my cousins, we heard knocking at the front door.

My uncle went to open it. The village chief and two policemen with light gray uniforms were standing in front.

"What's going on?" Uncle Lishui asked. He knew his name was on the police's list of Falun Gong practitioners.

"Don't worry," the village chief assured him. He put on his glasses, narrowed his eyes, and examined the list of names. "I'm helping Officers Zhang and Liu from the county police station confiscate the Falun Gong books and other materials."

"None of us have done anything wrong," Laoye said. "It's just a form of exercise." He tried to smile to ease the tension, but the officers did not smile back.

One of the officers took off his hat and revealed a glossy sheen of sweat on his forehead. "We're just following orders."

"Hand over the books and DVDs, Lishui," Officer Zhang urged my uncle. He had to play tough in front of the policemen even though he and my uncle were friends.

Uncle retreated to his bedroom to fetch the materials. He took out a bag of books and DVDs and a red lotus-shaped cushion. He handed over the articles to the officers.

The policemen walked around the house to complete their routine check of every corner. When they were done, the sweaty officer said to my grandfather, "I hear you're a Communist Party member. Falun Gong definitely conflicts with that. Be careful."

"Yes," his colleague said, looking around the room at us, "you are smart people. You know everything will be fine if you stand in line with the government. But if you stand against us, you will mess up your life and your children's. Be a good example for the rest of the *lǎobǎixìng*, eh." They proceeded to walk out.

I saw them throw the books and DVDs into the trunk.

"Were they warning me?" Laoye cried after they left. "When I was on the battlefield, their fathers were just crying babies! Who the hell are they to tell *me* what to do?"

Uncle Lishui led him to a chair to calm down. "Just give them what they want. If people ask, just say you don't practice it anymore. Easy..."

"Why did you hand the books over?" Laoye yelled. "Didn't you spend money on those books?"

"Father, please. We could have been arrested."

"What law have we broken?"

"The Communist Party is the law. If they say it's black, then it will never be white."

Laoye sat back in his chair, annoyed. They never found the books hidden under his quilts.

★   ★   ★

Tens of thousands of Falun Gong members were arrested and tortured. Some members were arrested and sentenced to jail without trial, or sent to "re-education" camps where they had to work for as long as fifteen hours a day without rest, and could be beaten for not finishing, or for no reason at all.

They were treated like slaves and fed bread, gruel, and watery soup. When questioned by international media and human rights organizations, the Chinese government said the crackdown was China's internal affair, and other nations had no right to intervene. In other words, they should mind their business.

Laoye still practiced secretly in his room but people like Kuoxiang never hid. She and other members would protest at the Tianjin municipal government building and planned to take trips to Beijing. Before they could get there the first time, they were stopped by police and locked in a local prison, without trial, for three years.

CHAPTER SEVEN

The Girl with Big Feet

Before Yunxiang could take the *gaokao*, the college entrance exam, local police came to our home for an investigation. They wanted to make sure our family was not involved with any political movements that threatened the Communist Party. If so, Yunxiang would not be able to attend college. Laoye and Uncle Lishui had to have their fingerprints taken and sign a letter stating that they were no longer members of Falun Gong. With that, Yunxiang passed the investigation.

Yunxiang was accepted to the same military university as our cousin Zheng. Baba was so proud that he posted the admission letter on the wall in our kitchen.

Congratulations on joining the
People's Liberation Army College

To fulfill the responsibility to protect the motherland, Comrade Yunxiang from Lutai Town, the Ninghe District of Tianjin municipal city, voluntarily applied to attend PLA College. He has passed the test hosted by the Tianjin student recruitment committee, and has been accepted. Yunxiang will attend our university on September 1, 2002.

My mother suggested we spend a few weeks of vacation in Chaoyang that summer. I teased her, saying that she just wanted the villagers to fawn over Yunxiang's good news, but I understood. It had been seven years since we left Chaoyang after her fight with Grandfather Wengui, and Mom wanted to give the villagers a renewed sense of our family. Now that Yunxiang was going to a prestigious university, all the heartache she endured had been worth it.

I was happy for Yunxiang too. The People's Liberation Army (PLA) is well respected by the Chinese. After the Communist Party won the civil war in 1949, the government and military formed an unshakable union—as bonded as fish to water. Although rich people were admired, the army ranked even higher in China. The PLA takes marching orders only from the Communist Party.

Both Yunxiang and our cousin Zheng were accepted through the help of my mother's younger brother, Siyong, who was a member of the military. Of course, Yunxiang and Zheng got high scores on the *gaokao*, but without that connection, there would have been no way to be admitted into a top military university, which was free and guaranteed jobs postgraduation.

When I was young, my happiest times were when Uncle Siyong visited. His unit was based in Beijing and he always wore his uniform when he visited us in Caiyuan. His appearance would attract a crowd, and a flock of cheering people would escort him all the way to his parents' door. I'd walk by Uncle Siyong's side to show off. He was our hero. I was happy that Yunxiang was officially going to bring back honor to my mother's name, and to her place in the village.

More importantly, Yunxiang's success in the gaokao gave me some hope. If I worked hard, I could also go to a university one day, maybe a better one. My entire life was a secret competition with my brother—as if as a girl, the second child that cost my mom so much, I had to prove to her that I could bring as much or even more honor to her.

After Yunxiang left for school, my grandparents moved in with us. Laolao accepted the situation and moved into Yunxiang's room, but Laoye had a harder time adjusting to town life and went back to the village.

I went to middle school that autumn and grew even more dissatisfied with my education, which mainly consisted of grand histories of influential men.

To entertain myself, I'd spend hours in the library reading folktales and researching oral histories. I wanted to learn the history of regular people like me and my family, not the martyrs China had invented. I was fed up with the same patriotic tales. I started to doubt whether those stories were true at all, or to what degree. I often saw a different, sometimes even contradictory, point of view between the history books and history told through the lives of ordinary people I knew.

One day I was reading in bed next to Laolao while she ate sunflower seeds. My history teacher wanted me to submit

an essay for a competition. I decided to write about someone I knew, someone who was not talked about in history
books but who had experienced it firsthand.

I was in the middle of deep thought about who when
Laolao suddenly said, "Your feet are big." She touched my
toes. Laolao was in good spirits these days, although she'd
cough and still had to put a blanket over herself even with
the slightest breeze. "Today you girls have big feet, like
you're showing off your freedom," she joked. "Is it revenge
on us old women?"

I laughed. I knew Laolao liked my big feet. "Big feet are
a good sign. It means that you will grow tall into your future," she'd often say.

Laolao had big feet, too, and so did my mom. Laolao said
her own would have been a blessing if she had been a working woman, but she had never been able due to a lifetime of
ill health. She said Mom's big feet made her a better farmer.
Small feet were for rich women; they were the only ones
who needed to be beautiful. Big feet were more practical, allowing us to walk faster and more easily on country roads.
She explained that, in the past, women's feet were bound
to be made smaller. If you were a girl of four or five years
old from a well-off family, your parents would bind your
feet. They'd take the feet, bend the bones, tightly wrap them
with cloth, and put them under a stone for days and nights
to ensure they would never grow. The "three-inch golden
lotuses" were considered attractive, though they were ex-
tremely painful, and limited movement. To walk, these
women had to have good balance and avoid getting trapped
in the mud. Therefore, these women stayed home most of

the time, which was considered a female virtue and a sign of privilege.

I had never talked to Laolao about it or met my great-grandmother, but I knew she'd had bound feet. Mom told me she complained about them often. At night, she would remove the cloth binding and soak them in warm water. This reminded me of Laolao's saying: "I am weak as a lady, but humble as a maid." In traditional Chinese culture, women who looked pale and weak were considered beautiful. If Laolao had been born to a rich family, her fair skin and frail, slender figure would match her status. However, she was a farmer's daughter. On the farms, to be rough and stout was more fitting, if not beautiful.

Although foot binding had been banned long ago, people hadn't changed their views so much on beauty. Growing up, words like *pretty* or *keai* were never used to describe me. I had small eyes, whereas big eyes were considered nice-looking. I had freckles. My nose was too flat, and I was short. My relatives always joked that I was adopted, because I didn't inherit my mom's beauty. At times, I'd stand in front of a mirror and imagine how I'd feel if I had a face like Chunting's, which everyone in the family adored. Laolao never made jokes about my looks, she always complimented me, especially my feet.

I decided that I would write about Laolao for my project. I put down my book and moved closer to her, and told her.

"I'm just an illiterate old village woman. That's all there is to the story!" Laolao protested as she spit shells into a plastic bag. People of her generation didn't like to talk about the past. They chose to forget.

I smiled and got my pen ready to take notes anyway.

Laolao came close to having her feet bound, my essay started.

In 1911, the Xinhai Revolution spread like wildfire from the south to the rest of the country. It ended the Qing dynasty in 1912, and the new government became devoted to eliminating traditions they believed to be feudal and backward; foot binding was one of them.

The revolutionary order did not make its way to Laolao's village until the mid-1920s, when Laolao had just begun having her feet bound: Her parents wanted their four-year-old to have tiny feet—a prerequisite for a good marriage. Laolao's feet were tightly wrapped with a white cloth eight feet long and four inches wide. To force the four toes (except the big toe) to point down toward the sole of the foot, her mother and grandmother used both their hands to pull the cloth tight. At first, my grandmother, Little Guiqin, was told to practice walking so she could get used to the pain. The torture lasted for a few hours a day. She'd painfully and slowly pace up and down the yard. She'd cry and cry but then she got lucky. Less than a week after the initial binding, revolutionaries put a stop to the tradition. Gradually, Guiqin's feet began to recover.

★   ★   ★

Laolao's stories helped me to understand more about her own life but also about others of her generation that are not written about in history books.

In the 1920s, Chinese warlords—independent military

commanders who ruled various parts of the country—were fighting with each other for power and territory. The Nationalist Party launched a military expedition against them to unify the country. The expedition began from the nationalists' base in Guangdong and spread all the way to the northern cities.

One day, when Laolao was five years old, news spread that an army would stop at her village on their way to Dongbei, the northeastern provinces. The villagers didn't know to which warlord the army belonged, but they knew it was best not to deal with the soldiers, who were no different from bandits.

Laolao's father decided the family should hide in his cousin's village for a few days. They left enough food for their donkey and tied him to a fence in the yard. But her father was still worried. After three days, he said the army must have left and that it would be safe to sneak back home via a secret path running through the wheat field, which was tall enough to hide him. He set off with only his friend, but, unbeknownst to them, two soldiers were on the other side. When they spotted my great-grandfather, they started to shoot. His friend lay down in a ditch, but my great-grandfather ran. The men shouted at him to stop, but he kept running. Then a gunshot hit him, *boom*, and he fell down dead.

The two soldiers left him lying there, and after they were gone, my great-grandfather's friend sneaked back to Laolao's family with the news, but he was unsure about the identity of the shooters. Were they local gangsters wearing looted uniforms? The nationalist soldiers coming from the south? Or locally hired soldiers belonging to the warlord? It didn't matter: A poor man's death meant nothing in a time when countless people died in the war every day. The only condolence from the local government was a coffin made from cheap willow wood.

With his death, the family had no adult men left. There were just two widows at the head—Laolao's grandmother, who had lost her husband a few years before, and Laolao's mother, who had five young daughters, including a one-month-old. No men meant no stable income. Her mother and grandmother fed the whole family by selling hand-made baskets and mats.

*   *   *

At fifteen, Laolao married my grandfather. Their wedding night was the first day they met. It was not her decision to marry him, or not—it was arranged. He left home one year later for a business in the Tianjin capital, leaving her behind to take care of his three younger brothers, along with his five aunts, who visited often.

"At twenty-one, I gave birth to your oldest uncle, Shoukui. And then four other sons came one after another, then your mother…"

"Wait, no, Mom has three older brothers." I stopped and put my pen aside.

"I gave birth to nine children in the next twenty years, but two died. I never told you."

I was thirteen years old, but my eyes started to tear up. Laolao never showed her emotions in front of her children and grandchildren. She said she had stopped crying long ago. She wiped my eyes with her handkerchief and I continued writing her story, which I encouraged her to continue.

The newborn mortality rate in China back then was high. One of her sons died from pneumonia and the other of meningitis. She locked herself in a storage room for several days to mourn them.

In traditional Chinese culture, babies who died were not considered family members. They were *tăozhài gui,* "little ghosts" who came to the family to collect "emotional debts"—their parents must have hurt them in their last life, so they return to make them sad. The two little boys were wrapped in reed mats, covered by pink and deep purple morning glory blossoms, and buried at the riverbank. No one spoke about them again.

My grandmother found some relief after she and my grandfather managed to purchase their own farmland. They had saved for years, but only three days after they received the title documents, the Communists announced that all land now belonged to the public, as part of the People's Commune movement. Their new home became the public kitchen, their land confiscated. I had heard only some bits of this story before, told by other family members. But it was so different to hear it from Laolao. I realized that, once again, my grandmother had had no say in her destiny.

Laolao described to me how riddled with worry her mind became at that time. Many of her days and nights were spent in fear. Her home had been "borrowed." What was next? she wondered. Villagers said the children would be the next. *Soon they will be shared too*, the women would say. *The government will take our children away, to raise them in a collective camp where they will learn how to be the "successors to the Communist cause."*

It sounded dramatic but so did a famine, and that had proven to be possible.

A few years after the war, during the Great Famine (1959–1961), anything alive and breathing was caught and eaten by the villagers—first wild rabbits, snakes, dogs, and later, rats and insects. When the grain sacks were empty in the public kitchen, it would be a long time before the government sent the next batch. Laolao would take the children to dig up grass to eat. Many villagers did this, and soon the farmland was just dirt, so Laolao would peel bark from the willow trees. She'd boil this for hours, cut it into pieces, mix it with a special flour made from smashed corncobs, and steam it. Thanks to the bark and corncobs, they made it through the worst days.

I listened to Laolao and took notes, pushing her for more details even when her voice got low.

In the winter of 1963, Laolao got pregnant and decided that she would give away her newborn son. They were totally impoverished, and she wanted him to be with a family that could afford to look after him. "But when the baby smiled and his fingers touched my face, my heart melted and I couldn't do it."

She tugged on a pillow and lay down. "I need to rest," she said. "I'm tired." I hugged her. We agreed to continue the project later. I knew talking about the past was hard for her. I felt grateful that she had opened up to me, and it made me cherish her even more. I also felt a twinge of guilt about how little I had considered what she and my grandfather had gone through. They spoke in pieces and fragments, but I don't know that I was ever listening much to them.

Growing up, I watched Laolao live so frugally. She didn't have fancy clothes. She never threw away a piece of fabric. She spent her time mending broken things, from sheets and jackets to socks, gloves, and towels. Even when life improved in the 1990s, if I left a few grains of rice in my bowl, she would eat them herself, reaching over with her chopsticks.

"When your mother was your age, she ate rice only in her dreams," said Laolao.

I used to put my hands over my ears to protest against these old tales of hardship.

"Laolao, there's no need to save every single thing," I'd say, grabbing plates with oil left behind before she poured hot water in them to make "soup." I took for granted that life would get better and better for me. Laolao's life had not taken the same path; for her, it had become harder.

Yet watching how she lived embarrassed me.

"What if there's a war and we're faced with starvation again tomorrow?" Laolao would ask me.

"Impossible!" I'd shout. "Times have changed. The government doesn't have the same sort of control anymore."

Life had taught Laolao that stability was not guaranteed; nothing was permanent, and that it would be foolish to trust in anything unconditionally. These were lessons my school textbooks couldn't teach me about China.

I went back to my room to begin writing. My family's past was like a rusted box locked in a corner, covered with dust. It was so heavy and worn that nobody wanted to touch it. I knew what to expect inside: endless pain. Yet it was only by opening it that I could understand my family, and myself.

*   *   *

I never had the chance to finish my history project with Laolao. She became ill and insisted on returning to Caiyuan in the winter. She had a cold for a long time, and grew so weak that her lungs became infected. I was worried about her. She coughed and coughed, and sweat accumulated on her brow. She vomited up whatever she ate and had to get a nutrient injection to maintain what little strength she had left.

"If I die, I want to die at home in Caiyuan, not in this town," Laolao said.

I didn't like it when she talked like that. She had been ill my entire life, but I had never expected her to die. I would never be ready to lose her.

She also got into the habit of talking to herself in whispers that winter. At first it was just occasional and everyone ignored it, but then she began to do it daily, even when there were guests around. I couldn't fathom her death, but I grew more and more worried that she was losing her mind.

That strange winter, people in town also talked about a disease from Guangdong, China's most southern coastal province. Called SARS, or severe acute respiratory syndrome, it was spreading throughout China and killing people. But without the government's formal confirmation that it was a deadly epidemic, most people dismissed it as a rumor.

My friends and I worried about it a lot because it was said that you could catch the disease by talking to somebody who was infected. You'd then get a fever and cough, your muscles would ache, and your immune system would break down in a matter of days. Many felt it was nature's revenge on the Guangdong people because they were believed to be savages who still ate wild animals like snakes and monkeys—which after the Great Famine was seen as inhumane. People had to piece together their own stories, but the government prevented the real story from existing.

For months, we were kept uninformed. That year the National People's Congress had received international recognition because China was finally putting in place a new government after President Jiang Zemin's ten-year term. Officials were worried that releasing information about SARS would sully the party's image. Their delayed reaction, and the withholding of information or suggestions on how to prevent the disease, increased our sense of panic. Information about SARS was censored, and no journalist was allowed to report on it.

But fear of SARS didn't wait for the government's approval to spread.

In Lutai, every family scrambled to the shops for vinegar.

The vapor was said to help protect you from the disease. *Banlangen*, a common Chinese herbal medicine used for curing colds, was sold for ten times its normal price. The streets and markets were often empty; people wanted to avoid crowds and infection. What scared me most was not the disease itself, but the horrid atmosphere it created.

A shadow of death was cast over my town and many others. The disease felt like an invisible monster, lurking in the shade, that could jump out to eat me at any time. My family and I were helpless because we didn't know what exactly it was and so had no means to defend ourselves. Mom put vinegar in iron bowls to evaporate on the stove, and only when the rooms were full of the smell did I feel safe.

It was not until late April that CCTV's *Xinwen Lianbo* began to report on the SARS outbreak. The anchors announced that in the capital city of Beijing alone, more than one hundred cases were being logged each day. Uncle Si-yong called us and said his compound was sealed off and that no one was allowed in or out. Nobody was allowed to leave the compound unless for urgent reasons that had to be approved by the chief. Beijing schools were closed, and students had to study at home via online videos. Since there weren't any officially reported infection cases in our hometown, schools in Lutai and nearby villages were still open. But our teachers didn't give homework in order to "relieve pressure on students and improve their immunity," as instructed by the local education bureau chief.

Every morning before we entered the classroom, a teacher in charge would put an electric thermometer on our head. Our temperature was recorded and noted down in a chart for the school hospital. Whenever anyone felt a little bit uncomfortable, no matter whether it was a teacher or student, they were urged by the headmaster to leave school immediately without needing any approval. Some of my friends faked illness just so they could play hooky.

I was in seventh grade, and normally my classes would start at 7:30 a.m. and end at 5:30 p.m., but now I left school at 3:30 p.m. at the latest. I wasn't happy at all with the new schedule. Our final exam was approaching, and we were really behind. My score on the exam would determine whether I could go on to the top-ranking class next year. Students from wealthy families had tutors, but my family couldn't afford that.

People didn't believe it when the premier announced on television that SARS was now under control. At the entrance to Caiyuan, people volunteered to take turns standing guard, in case any strangers tried to get in. The government absurdly sent fitness equipment to the village, which was placed in the chief's office to encourage people to exercise, as if that could really prevent SARS.

During my weekend visits to the village, I watched TV with Laolao and we'd listen to updates about the SARS situation in Beijing. She kept a bowl of hot, boiled vinegar in the corner of every room. When the anchors revealed the number of newly infected and the death toll, she furrowed her eyebrows. "Siyong called, but I can't tell if he's really well or not," she said to me. She became increasingly worried, so much so that I feared she was growing paranoid. Yet now I understood why she would; she had lost two other sons.

Once spring came, we had news from Siyong less frequently, which made Laolao sleepless. She insisted that her other children call their brother. My mom tried to comfort her, saying, "Mother, don't worry. They're very safe in the PLA compound. You should trust the country."

"Trust the country?" Laolao said. "Nobody in the village trusts the country more than me. I've trusted the country my whole life, but has the country taken care of me?"

It was rare to hear Laolao talking so heatedly.

"This country took everything away from me. What have I got in return? I got to know the taste of grass and tree bark. In trusting the country, my son Lishui served as a Red Guard and had to do many things against his will, but nobody's paying for his retirement."

Laolao had never complained. She was obedient and quiet, a person who took whatever life gave her and did what women were supposed to do without question. To hear her say these things hurt me. I felt her anger. It was not until she was this old, almost dying, that she could speak out.

"I don't care about China anymore. I only care about my children. Call me selfish." Laolao was so emotional she started to cough.

"Siyong is fine," my mom said, patting Laolao's back to ease her cough. Uncle Lishui pulled the blanket up over her.

"If he's fine, why can't he come home?" Laolao cried. "He said he didn't have much work recently."

"To avoid infection," Mom said to console her. "Staying in the compound will keep him safe."

The management in a PLA compound was strict. If enforcers said nobody was allowed out, then that was it and Siyong had to obey, but Laolao couldn't understand it.

That evening, to avoid upsetting Laolao, we didn't turn on the television, and the next day, Uncle Lishui called in the doctor to give her an intravenous drip. She was delirious again. In the past fifty years, her health had gone from bad to worse, but she'd only go to the hospital if the village doctor couldn't cure her symptoms. Hospitals were expensive—they still are—and farmers never had health insurance. The village doctor was self-taught and was also a fellow farmer. I always felt embarrassed when his mud-stained shoes entered my grandparents' house, but he probably had no time to change clothes between being a doctor and working his cornfield. He was nice, but I wished for more for Laolao. If she had been as privileged as a government worker, for example, she would have had medically trained and qualified doctors to heal her long ago. At least that is how I felt. What a different life she could have had. At that time, I was more certain than ever that being poor was the most unfortunate thing in the world. It would literally kill my grandmother.

Mom had been right about wanting more than a rural *hukou* for me, and about moving us to Lutai. Yet I was still considered a farmer's daughter, and had no other option but to study hard, pass my *gaokao* to be admitted to a good college, find a decent job in the city, and bury my village identity once and for all.

A few days later, Aunt Zhirong heard Laolao muttering

in her bed. "What is it, Mother?" Zhirong asked. She assumed her mother-in-law was having a nightmare.

Laolao opened her eyes. "There's poison in the drip."

"No..."

"You all lie to me. Where's Siyong? He is the only one who doesn't lie to me."

Her mind was gone. Laolao didn't remember that she had just talked to Siyong on the phone. Soon after, she would mistake me for Chunting. She began referring to my mom and my uncles as evil demons. Strangely, though, her coughing and asthma had disappeared. And her eyes burned with a fierce, sharp gaze.

When Chunting and I went into her room, she was irritable and shouted loudly about strange things. If I tried to hold her hands, she'd throw my own off her own and shout: "I'm not human. I'm a yellow weasel. I'm here in this old lady's body just to make a mess for your family."

Chunting and I would look at each other, not sure what to say.

At first, we all thought she was suffering from temporary hallucinations and would soon recover, but she only got worse. By summer, on most days, Laolao didn't recognize me. Once, when it was just Laolao and me alone at home, she put on a fisherman's hat, jumped from her bed to the ground, and rushed out the gate. I chased after her.

She stopped in the yard to break a tree branch. "This is my sword," she said, waving it at me. "I see you, demon! As a messenger from the gods, I'm obliged to kill you!"

I was startled, and though I knew she was sick, I felt

hurt. Uncle Lishui suddenly appeared and pulled her back from me.

⋆   ⋆   ⋆

Everyone began to gossip about Laolao's newfound strength—how she could now hop out of bed with the swiftness of a cat. It didn't take long before the whole village was talking about her: The *huángshǔláng*, the yellow weasel, was haunting her.

The *huángshǔláng* was once believed to have the power to haunt people, especially women, and encourage them to do absurd, brutal, or evil things. This is what the old people said.

While I was growing up, of the many stories Laolao told me, my favorites were about the *huángshǔláng*. Because Laolao had been too sickly to go to school and stayed indoors most days, stories were her way to explore. Tales of yellow weasels were handed down to her by her mother, whose own mother had passed them on to her.

When I was about six years old, my family spent Spring Festival Eve at my grandparents' house. We put two tables near the stove. My mom, her little sister, Aunt Shuhua, and Uncle Lishui and his wife, Aunt Zhirong, sat at one table, making steamed buns and dumplings. At the other table, Laoye played Chinese chess with his sons, surrounded by my older cousins. Chunting and I sat with Laolao on the *kang*, the traditional-style heated bed warmed by pipes running underneath. When Laolao was speaking, we'd become so absorbed in the story that we wouldn't even hear our aunts calling for us to come and taste the dumplings.

"In the village where I was born," Laolao would begin, "a woman had a fight one day with her new daughter-in-law. When the hens clucked, she'd ask her daughter-in-law to fetch the eggs, but the young woman came back and said, 'There was nothing in the coop!' For the first three days, the old woman believed her daughter-in-law, but after the fourth day, she became suspicious. By the fifth day, she concluded that her daughter-in-law was stealing the eggs, and told her so. To prove herself innocent, the young woman hid behind the coop before the hens clucked. The hens proceeded to cluck and lay eggs, but within seconds, two weasels jumped into the coop, grabbed the eggs, and quickly jumped back out. The young woman couldn't believe it! The next day she forced her mother-in-law to come with her to see. The old woman finally stopped cursing her."

Laolao said weasels were smart and liked to play tricks on people. They'd do things like imitate roosters crowing to deceive people about the time. The most mysterious thing about the weasels was how they could possess women like spirits, making them do crazy things.

Laolao believed these stories, as well as those about gods and fairies. A week before the Spring Festival, Laolao would place fruits, steamed buns, and candies in front of the shrine for the *zaowangye*, the kitchen god, to protect the family from harm. On the night before the Spring Festival, she'd put portraits of *menshen*, the gate gods, on her gate. The two gods had red faces, round eyes, and raised eyebrows. They held swords and stood ready to fight off evil spirits.

My parents' generation also had crazy stories, which they often used as ways of explaining things.

One Saturday, when I arrived at Laolao's house from Lutai, Aunt Zhirong grabbed my arms to stop me from entering Laolao's room.

"Hush, Chaoqun, Laolao's sleeping, finally! Your uncles are on their way to the *daxian*, the witch in Fengtai Town. Let's hope we can get her to help."

This sort of talk was nonsense to me, but Zhirong said the witch was their last hope for healing Laolao. "None of us would like to believe it, but what else can we do?" Aunt Zhirong gently tapped my shoulders.

She then pulled up her sleeve and showed me her wrist, which was bruised with the imprint of teeth.

That morning, when Aunt Zhirong had offered a bowl of congee—a kind of porridge made of rice or other grains—to Laolao, she grabbed the bowl and threw it to the floor like a madwoman. She then pulled Zhirong over by the hand and bit down hard on her.

The doctor said Laolao had cerebellar atrophy, which meant that part of her brain was damaged and that's why she had trouble behaving normally. The explanation was that psychological trauma and physical sickness together had caused her mental breakdown. The psychological trauma most intrigued me. I believed that what killed my grandmother was how much she had suffered by coming of age as a woman in a time and in a country that had been so politically turbulent, and often life-threatening. There was no cure.

★　　★　　★

When Laolao fell asleep, my heart felt as if it would never recover. I sat near her bed for a long time. I had so many questions for her, but she was no longer able to answer them. It was not always easy for me to understand her, even after I knew more of her story. She was sixty-five when I was born, and her life remained dramatically different from mine.

I would never forgive her for not helping Mom get into college, as much as I loved Laolao. In the 1960s, although China advocated gender equality and encouraged women to become as educated as men, it was not a big deal if girls didn't go to school. The old ways died hard: Women were supposed to get married, not educated. Grandmother had not been educated, and she created the same fate for Mom, who didn't start school until she was nine years old. She was in the same class as her younger brother, Siyong. After ninth grade, although Mom was a better student, Laolao and Laoye let Siyong go to high school and kept my mother at home.

"That was so unfair!" I said loudly to my grandmother when I heard this.

Laolao was shocked by my reaction. To her, it made perfect sense. "We didn't have any other choice," she said finally.

"You did have a choice, but you gave the chance to your son."

"That was not a choice, Chaoqun. How could I let a girl steal my boy's opportunity? Women go with their husbands;

that's the law of nature. She would be fine; he would not. Have you ever heard of it being the other way around?"

"It would not be *stealing*, Laolao," I said, flinging my hands in the air. "The opportunity belonged to my mother! She was a better student."

Grandmother was not moved by what I said. Her eyes turned back to the socks she was sewing, and she said calmly, "You're lucky. When you go to school, you're not competing with your brother. Make full use of that opportunity, little girl."

At those times, Laolao disappointed me. I wondered why my grandmothers and other women of their generation safeguarded the male-dominated social system. Why had they shown no mercy to their daughters on life-changing decisions like education and career opportunities? I knew they loved their girls. If Laolao had one piece of candy, she gave it only to her granddaughters, after the boys had left. That was her way of loving us. But when it came to dreams, future, fortune, and status, only boys qualified. Why couldn't she see this wasn't right? This plagued me.

In traditional Chinese culture, if the boys were successful, they could bring money to the family, and the family's status was based on their sons' achievements. Investment in daughters equaled investment in another family. And it was not the wives and mothers who had a final say. But the rules in China were changing. Like my mom, women had begun working outside the home. Mom had been my inspiration throughout in all of this because she had chosen her own way and played by her own rules. After Laolao's death, I started making plans to take it a step further.

Laolao died on December 24, 2003. Her body was cremated; her ashes temporarily stored in a local columbarium—where boxes of ashes were kept—until her husband, my grandfather, died and the ashes of the two of them could be buried together in the same tomb. I tried to forget how terrified she looked in her last days and remembered instead her gentle smile. As I sat by her dying side, I felt warmth in my heart when I thought of the time I had tried to teach her to read and write. It was when she was living with us that I proposed the idea, my eyes peering at her over a book.

"Laolao," I said, "if you could read, your life would be better."

She laughed and said: "Reading at my age is foolish," before returning to her needlework. But I insisted that we give it a try. Every evening, Mom and I sat with Laolao, teaching her five characters.

"This is *ren*—human—Laolao, the character looks like a human standing on his two legs." One day I took out the book I had used in first grade, and sat beside her in bed, drawing the characters in a notebook.

"It's not that difficult," Laolao said with a smirk. She took a pencil and followed me in writing down the next character.

"With two straight lines on *ren*, then it's *tian*, heaven." I started to make upstrokes. "You know heaven is above the head."

"Yes, that's what the character for heaven should look like," she said, nodding. Laolao took the book and flipped through it. "If I learned five characters a day, I would know a lot of characters in a year. Could I read a newspaper by then?"

It was like a nice dream; I smiled again at the thought of what I had achieved in just receiving that comment from her.

Sadly, the study sessions stopped when she got ill, and they never started again.

Six years later, during an auspicious time when we could all gather, our family took her box of ashes and buried them next to her husband. Finally, Laolao could rest in peace.

PART II

Third Generation

CHAPTER EIGHT

Chunting Gets a Boyfriend

Chunting and I were lying in bed, tossing and turning on a hot summer's night. We were older now—teenagers—and often restless about different matters than our five-year-old selves. Struggling to fall asleep, we decided to chat, which only made us more awake.

"I'm in love," said Chunting in the darkness.

I jumped up and turned on the desk lamp. At sixteen, Chunting's confession was big news—epic.

"I'm your favorite cousin," I said. "You must tell me everything—all the details."

I dragged her to the chairs at the window.

"Fine, fine!" Chunting readily gave in.

The boy's name was Jiaming. Fair-skinned and with long hair, he was the quietest in her class. He was not tall but had a sweet smile. One day, she found a letter on blue paper with neat handwriting in her desk. It had been folded into a heart shape. It was from Jiaming, asking Chunting to be his girlfriend.

"Wow!" I almost screamed before I realized how late it was. "And then you said yes?"

"I did!"

"What does it feel like to be in love?"

She shrugged and blushed a little. "I don't know."

"Your school allows dating? If my teachers found out any of us were dating, we'd be in so much trouble."

"Well, it's not really allowed, but you know, no one sticks to the rules in my high school. It's a vocational high, and nine out of ten have boyfriends or girlfriends," said Chunting in a tone that made me feel I was out of touch with reality. "You've never had a boyfriend at school?".

"No."

The bright moon outside cast shadows of tree branches waving gently over Chunting's face as I poured out question after question that night: "How do you date? How does it feel to have a boyfriend in your class? When you hold hands, does it feel like what we read in novels: like a little deer roaming in your stomach?"

I was three months older than Chunting and had always been a bit more advanced than she was—from learning to speak to using chopsticks first. But this time, on love, Chunting had won.

My mom said Chunting and I were so close we could communicate before either of us could talk. We babbled on and on, and laughed at things only the two of us could understand. She was the prettiest girl in our family, with big black eyes and long eyelashes. Her lips were cherry red, and her curved eyebrows looked like two half-moons on her round face. With her bob haircut, she looked like a

Japanese doll. Everyone always complimented her parents on her beauty in contrast to how they reacted to me. People would say: "Look how pretty your cousin is. Are you adopted?" I could not tell if they were joking or serious, but I'd go along with it and tell them Chunting was a white swan and I was an ugly duckling.

Things changed when we went to school. Family friends and relatives still said how much prettier Chunting was, but they cared more about how well I was doing academically. My good grades were fueled by my competitive nature. It wasn't just a race to beat my brother, but also my pretty cousin and my Lutai classmates. I had neither a beautiful face nor an urban *hukou*, so I told myself I had to be good at something to be equal to them, or even superior. My uncles and aunts brought me up when they talked to their children. "Can't you learn from cousin Chaoqun?"

Chunting struggled with studying, and it hurt her confidence, making her self-conscious and shy.

Though she studied in Caiyuan, and I in Lutai, we spent almost every weekend together. We shared all our girlish secrets and plans for the future; Chunting would be a film star, and I would be a singer. Neither of us knew anyone who led such lavish lives. Our lives were plain, but without worry, until the day we were put at our first crossroads.

After nine years of both primary and middle school, I was accepted to a prestigious high school in Lutai, while Chunting's score was too low for any high school except a vocational one called Ninghe Technical Secondary.

When higher education was not common, many job opportunities came from vocational school training in cooking, hairstyling, factory management, or even teaching. But in the late 1990s, things shifted. As China expanded its higher education system, a four-year university degree became the basic requirement for most companies hiring white-collar workers. Parents believed the time and money spent on vocational schools to be a waste of money. Stereotypes about kids who attended vocational high schools began to flourish: It was alleged that they fought and smoked a lot, that the girls were obsessed with makeup and *zao lian*, a "relationship that comes too early."

But if not vocational school, what could a sixteen-year-old girl from a village do? Uncle Lishui was reluctant to pay the 4,000-yuan tuition fee each year for Chunting, but he still did it. He also decided that she should study electronic engineering, which he hoped would help her find work after graduation. In China, it's common for parents to make decisions for their children about everything, from what majors they choose at college, to what jobs they take, to what kind of man their daughter should date, and the best age for a young couple to start having babies. Although more and more of us millennials refuse and challenge our parents on these things, the pressure is always there. And, honestly, the kids usually listen, and obey.

Uncle's decision to enroll Chunting into a vocational high school was pragmatic. On the recruitment pamphlet, one line was in bold, red type: *Our school promises to assign a job to every student after they graduate.* Tianjin is one of the cities with the most foreign-invested factories, producing automobiles, cell phones, and technology. *Every factory needs talented people who understand the electrical*

machinery knowledge we teach in the three-year program.
Uncle Lishui showed this to his daughter as proof that it
was a good decision.

He believed in the advertisement.

I told Chunting adamantly that an engineering degree
from Ninghe Tech was not the answer. Though she knew
being a film star was unrealistic, her real passion was hair.
She loved to do mine and could do my makeup so that I
looked like the girls in *Ruili* magazine. I always burst into
laughter looking at my newly curled fringe and the blue
shadow on my eyelids.

"Aha, now you look like Ayumi Hamasaki," she'd say
with pride at making me up like the Japanese pop star.

I'd laugh and tease her: "You'd better get some proper
training."

I told Chunting to persuade Uncle Lishui that he should
change his mind, that she should become a stylist, and do
what truly interested her.

Uncle wouldn't hear of it. "Interests are just interests,"
he said. "Interests can't be traded for food. If you learned
makeup and hairdressing, there's no guarantee you'll find
a job."

"But factory work will be boring!" Chunting complained.

"A boring job is better than no job. If you had studied
harder, I would have paid whatever it cost to send you to a
proper three-year high school, but you didn't."

In the end, Chunting chose a "three-plus-two" program,
which meant that after three years in high school, she could
go to Tianjin for another two years of college. At our first
look at her courses, Chunting and I were annoyed and

alarmed: Basic Mechanics, Mechanical Drawing, Electrical Skills, Machine Control Principles, and so on.

What does any of this mean?! we wanted to scream.

Initially, Chunting was upset, but once she started, she was fine. There wasn't much pressure at her school. "I never knew life could be so easy," she told me. According to her, it seemed the students spent most of their time reading novels, passing notes to each other during lectures, and even chatting during class. The teachers didn't care so long as the students finished their assignments in the forty-five-minute time allotted.

Plus, Chunting got to live in a dormitory. I had never lived outside of home, so I begged her every weekend to tell me about it.

She and five other girls shared a 160-square-foot room. To save space, they slept on bunk beds. Chunting draped a pink curtain around her bottom bunk to create a little privacy. She taped up posters of Super Junior, her favorite South Korean boy band, on the wall beside her bed.

The girls were from nearby villages, so it was easy for her to fit in. Soon the six of them called each other *jie*, meaning "elder sister," and *mei*, meaning "younger sister." Over time they became like a little family.

The school forbade students from leaving the campus from Sunday night to Friday morning. On Friday afternoon almost everyone went home. Buses lined up on the street in front of the gate, the name of each village propped on the dashboards and visible through the windshield of every bus. After the first few weeks, Chunting began to enjoy her freedom so much that she stayed at school. She sometimes visited me in Lutai. After living in the village for sixteen years where there was nothing but farming, harvesting, watching TV, and gambling, Chunting couldn't get enough of the excitement of her independence and town life. I was a little jealous of her newfound independence!

She would hang out at the shopping center and go to places like the newly opened Shuoren restaurant, the most popular dating spot in town. People liked it because it had a European flair: black-and-white photos on dark red walls, with flower-patterned wall carvings, and a balcony. Chunting and I doubted anybody in town had ever been to Europe, but everyone seemed happy enough to assume that was how European restaurants looked.

She'd go to the Kawayi Headshot Shop, a Japanese photo studio. In the little booth, Chunting and her roommates would take photos, and for five yuan they could have headshots printed where their eyes appeared bigger and rounder, which is how town girls wanted to look.

She and her friends were just village girls in an expensive town, so they didn't have money for expensive products to look cool. They would find alternatives at Jia Le shopping center, a copycat of the French chain Carrefour. A Meili Lian lipstick, a Maybelline knockoff, was only ten yuan, and you could get the same outfit a celebrity wore for one hundred yuan at the South Korean fashion store. I felt like Chunting was living it up. She looked cool and was like an adult. Her parents and my parents worried that she was becoming overindulgent with her fashion sense and new town life full of restaurants and luxuries.

Unlike Laolao or my mom, my generation grew up with

China's embrace of commercialization. We didn't sew our own clothes—advertisements on television, in magazines, and on billboards told us what to buy, what to wear, and what to do. Pizza Hut and KFC had arrived in Lutai that spring, and young people packed inside to see if the pizza and fried chicken tasted as good as they looked on television.

My classmate Chen Lan even held her sixteenth birthday party at KFC. Her dad was a hotel manager, and talk of her party dominated the school for weeks. I wasn't invited, but it didn't take long before I knew all the details from my friends: Chen Lan's dad had ordered fried chicken, fries, burgers, and even coffee for twenty of her friends. Her mother had ordered a birthday cake from Meiweiduo, a new bakery. I felt so jealous when I saw the photos of them holding gigantic Coca-Cola bottles. I liked everything in KFC except the coffee. It was nothing like the instant Nescafé we drank at home.

Once, I complained with squinting eyes to the woman behind the counter at KFC, "Something's wrong with this coffee. It's bitter! I think it's bad."

She rolled her eyes. "Real coffee should be bitter."

As Chunting grew more obsessed with makeup and restaurants, I grew to love foreign movies. My parents allowed me to watch television only on the weekends or during breaks. I loved the American and Taiwanese films where a rich, simple, and well-educated man fell in love with a plain girl, and they lived a happy life together. These movies became the dating bible for us Chinese girls: A girl should be gentle and innocent, and the guy will protect her and finally marry her.

Mom said those shows were polluting my mind. Like any stubborn teenager, I ignored her. I liked them even though I knew they were cliché.

"Please, just let me enjoy my fantasies!" I'd shout from the sofa.

Mom grew up on stories of heroes and soldiers saving our country. I grew up with those grand stories, too, but also with Western fairy tales about Snow White and Cinderella. Mom's generation regarded "bitter eating" as normal and felt guilty about pleasure. Chunting and I—on the other hand—were more than fine with it.

*   *   *

The closer the summer holiday drew to an end, the more I'd feel my freedom dwindle. I was enrolled in the "experimental class" of a prestigious local high school—the No.1 Middle School—and my life was buried in studying. Founded in 1913, the school was one of the oldest in Tianjin. It held about five thousand middle and high school students, and had the best of everything: the largest collection of books in the library, the most up-to-date laboratory equipment, the most manicured soccer field and polished basketball courts, and the most highly qualified, experienced teachers. It was the greatest honor to study there. It gave me hope that one day I could be more than a village girl.

I was proud to wear the school badge—we were the most privileged people in Lutai.

We were the only high school in town with activities like art class and sports, but our schedule was bananas. From the first day, we were told that our futures depended totally on the highly competitive *gaokao*, the two-day exam that tests students in Chinese, English, math, and either science or social science. Each subject took three hours to complete. If you failed the *gaokao*, you failed in life, period. Only the *gaokao* scores mattered, not your personality, not your day-to-day performance, not your special talents.

First introduced in 1952, the exam was suspended during the Great Leap Forward, in part because the party wanted to send intellectual youth to the countryside so that they could contribute to patriotic collectivism, and in part to encourage colleges to accept working-class students. From 1966 to 1976, during the ten years of the Cultural Revolution, *gaokao* was stopped completely. Students were recommended rather than selected on the basis of exam results. Academic performance no longer mattered as much as connections to the party, so bright students like my dad were prevented from going. When the *gaokao* resumed in 1977, it caused great excitement, and a huge number of people who wanted to attend college, or who had been wanting for years to attend college, signed up to take the exam.

Some argue that the *gaokao* is an egalitarian way of formulating society. Actually, it's elitist: As the gap between rich and poor widens, students from wealthier families can attend better schools and get off to a better start and, hence, a better ending.

There have been controversial debates about eliminating the *gaokao*, but some experts say that to get rid of it could put poor children at an even bigger disadvantage. In a country where bribery is so common, the education system could be compromised.

Our entire education was tailored around the *gaokao*. Students had a weekend off only once a month. Classes started at 8 a.m., but we had to arrive at 7:30 a.m. for *zao zixi*, the morning self-study session. *Zixi* means self-study and *zao* means morning; *wan*, evening. *Zao zixi* was mostly used to read Chinese essays and memorize English vocabulary, because the teachers said students had the best memory in the morning.

"Unimportant" classes like music and fine art were cut from our schedules in the second year to make time for *gaokao*-related study. Physical education was the only exception because it helped to relax our brains...for the *gaokao*.

At the end of every month there was an exam, with the marks publicized and sent home to parents. Every year on the *gaokao* test-results day, students' names and the universities they were accepted to were posted on a huge board for all to see. The pressure was more than high; it was on fire. Unlike my cousin, I had no life.

And, most importantly, romance was banned!

To parents and teachers, *zao lian* led to lower grades or dropping out, or even to teenage pregnancy. "No *zao lian*" was written in our high school handbook alongside no fighting, no gambling, and no tattoos. If any students were found to be in a relationship, the teachers would scold them in front of their classmates and call the parents to take them home to reflect on their mistake.

I knew how ugly things could turn. A boy in my class, Wen, whose academic ranking was always among the top three, had set an example. Wen was expected to make it to

Tsinghua, the country's top university in Beijing. He had a girlfriend named Guixian, who was from his village. They never hid their relationship. Every day at lunchtime, Wen waited for Guixian outside her classroom. They studied together. Both lived on campus. After *wan zixi*, the evening self-study session, Wen walked hand in hand with his girlfriend to her dormitory before going to his and the couple were sometimes spotted kissing. Teenage girls were excited about such things. To me, their relationship was perfect.

Our mathematics instructor, Teacher Yun, was especially bothered by Wen's behavior.

Teacher Yun was in her early forties, and her small, piercing eyes looked as if they could see all your secrets. She talked so fast that if you were not 100 percent focused and had stopped listening for thirty seconds, you would never catch up again. Being called out by her was the worst. She liked to note down the names of students who broke the rules. Then, once a week, she would call all these students to her office and scold them one by one, in the meanest way you could imagine. To me and my classmates, nothing was worse than being humiliated in public. Her reputation preceded her, and gave her the magical ability to "turn a carnival into a temple," just by appearing at the door of a classroom. Many years later, I still wake from nightmares of Teacher Yun publicly scolding me for being late to class.

Teacher Yun scolded Wen many times, saying to him loudly in the corridor, "It's for your own good. You're going to Tsinghua and will have a bright future. What could a relationship do for you now?"

Wen wouldn't say a word and never seemed nervous

about this. When he returned to the classroom, we'd all raise our eyes from our work to look at him. He didn't stop seeing Guixian either. He was our hero.

Teacher Yun had informed Wen's and Guixian's parents about their relationship, but they were not against it. They had witnessed the two children growing up together and understood that they had a real connection. But the teachers still wanted them to split up. They were concerned about the example they were setting for the rest of us. If dating became the norm, as it was in Chunting's school, our teachers might lose control over us.

Teacher Yun liked the Chinese saying "Kill the chicken to set an example for the monkeys." She didn't give up, and tried another tactic, targeting Guixian. Once, when I went to hand in my homework at her office, I saw she was talking to Guixian. A dozen other people were in, hovering. Guixian's homeroom teacher was sitting beside Yun, whose eyes were daggers looking up and down at her.

"You're a bright girl. Why don't you respect yourself? Good girls are not flirtatious, and can control themselves."

Guixian began to cry.

It's so unfair, I thought. It reminded me of what happened to my mom in Chaoyang, where women were always the ones blamed. Though we were not in the village, it was no different for us here than it had been on the farm.

There was also the shame heaped on Guixian. For many generations—long, long ago, before my grandparents' generation—Chinese belief was and is that self-restraint in relationships and with regard to sex is a feminine virtue. Women should wait to be pursued by men and should play hard to get. In Chinese folktales, it is either prostitutes or evil-spirit animals, like the fox, who seduce men. This influenced us. A woman was expected to be submissive and asexual. Stories of men who despised and outed their new wives for not being virgins still made the news. When a man cheated on his wife, people were more tolerant of him but not his mistress. It was a double standard: For a man, having a lot of women was considered evidence of his charm, but for a woman, promiscuity stained her character.

*   *   *

Chunting's first love didn't last long.

Before they became boyfriend and girlfriend, Chunting and Jiaming could talk for hours about anything: Jay Chou's new album, or which kiosk had the best noodles. They talked all the time: during the class break, on the way to the cafeteria, even during classes. When they were not talking, they wrote little notes and passed them through rows of kids back and forth to each other.

But when they entered "relationship" status, in which neither of them had experience, suddenly something changed.

They didn't know what they were supposed to say or how to talk like lovers. Their friends made jokes and teased them about having a "relationship." No one really knew what it meant or how to have one.

We didn't have sex education in school or at home. As long as we avoided any talk of relationships, it was assumed that sex would not happen, and that accidental pregnancy would never be a problem.

At home, the most awkward moments were when I was watching television with my family and scenes of men and women being physically affectionate, or even just kissing, appeared. My parents would start talking over the sound to create a diversion, but it only increased my interest. When I was a little girl, I'd ask where I came from, and my mother would say, "I picked you out of a trash can."

Girls were to hang their drying underwear in a corner where nobody could see. They were to cover up and not show a lot of skin.

In my eighth-grade biology class when I was fourteen, we started learning about reproduction, and our teacher, a man in his twenties, suggested that we read the book by ourselves first. There were two drawings of genitals in the entire book.

There was also a paragraph about how a new life started when sperm met the egg. Our teacher then drew two pictures of men's and women's genitals on the blackboard. He said the only important part of this chapter to remember were the names: testicle, penis, vagina, ovary, and fallopian tube. I felt my face flush and quickly lowered my head. When I peeked up, I saw that my classmates had done the same.

The teacher finished the whole chapter in a single class. The part about menstruation and AIDS prevention was left for us to read for homework. He said the boys did not need to read the menstruation section. As for the AIDS section, he believed it just wasn't important. His face looked red the entire day. That was my only sex education, but I did realize from then on that I had come from a vagina, not a trash can.

Despite our sex-education class, my friends and I never learned anything about birth control. We were never taught how to use condoms or any other contraceptives, which are given out free—along with gynecological examinations— but are reserved only for married couples. At physical checkups, all doctors ask young women if they are married or not. They assume unmarried women are virgins and that a gynecological examination is unnecessary. Many unmarried women who want an exam but who are not virgins just lie and say they're married, to avoid an eye roll.

People do have sex, and women do get pregnant, but without proper sex education, the annual rate of abortion in China is more than ten million, and almost half of them are women under twenty-five. To the older generations, that statistic is a reflection of lax morality stimulated by the promiscuity shown on television, instead of the lack of sex ed.

But premarital sex has become more common, especially among my generation. A recent survey showed that 80 percent of people born between 1980 and 1989 working in Beijing don't oppose premarital sex.

All these conservative ideas on sex and relationships in our education were new. Before the 1950s, marriages like my grandmother's were arranged. It was common for people to marry young, sometimes at thirteen, if not younger, but the Communist Party outlawed the practice of arranged marriages. My parents' generation enjoyed the freedom of finding love and partnership of their own free will, though many still depended on matchmakers. They rarely dated and so, often, the only romantic relationship they had was with their husband or wife.

To my parents, a marriage was not a precious, loving experience but a responsibility and necessity. They thought puppy love a waste of time. A real relationship had structure: Two young people from families of similar socioeconomic backgrounds, once settled into their jobs, should wed. And not separate, regardless of whether you fought like dogs or not. Marriage was never personal, and divorce was always a disgrace.

But my generation found that modern life didn't fit with the old rules. Young people who studied and worked far away from home dated without their parents' permission. Divorce was no longer taboo. The older generation used to call divorced women "secondhand," having supposedly lost their "value," but now, even in the villages, a divorced young woman could still find suitors lined up at her parents' door.

Growing up in a time when the old traditions and values were still influential, yet new norms were becoming omnipresent, my classmates and I were confused. Pop songs, films, and novels made it seem as if love were the most beautiful thing in the world, and we didn't want to repress that feeling. Why people, like my uncle Jun and his wife, visibly hated each other but never divorced bewildered us. They said it was for their children's good, but their children told me they would prefer if their parents went their separate ways.

I began to understand that there was a big difference between human nature and what we were being taught about love.

Our teacher Ms. Dong would read and recite love poems from over two thousand years ago:

"Fair, fair," cry the ospreys
On the island in the river.
Lovely is this noble lady,
Fit bride for our lord.
In patches grows the water mallow;
To left and right one must seek it.
Shy was this noble lady;
Day and night he sought her.

Teacher Dong spoke admiringly of poetic love. *If our teachers forbid love so much, why don't they remove all the romantic poems from our curricula?* I'd wonder, why, quite to the contrary, romantic novels and poems amounted to a considerable portion of what we studied. I'd note down beautiful lines of poetry in a notebook, hoping to one day put them in letters to a special person:

To the Oak Tree

If I love you, I will never be a clinging trumpet creeper,
     using your high boughs to show off my height;
I will never be a spoony bird, repeating a monotonous
     song for green shade;
I must be a ceiba tree beside you.
Our roots melt underneath
Our leaves merge in clouds

"But you only learn the good side of love from these books," Teacher Dong warned. "Don't over-romanticize love. The best way to understand love is by practicing it," she said one day, hesitantly pushing her glasses up her nose, as if she had said too much. "But not now, of course."

I had something weighing on my mind: my first love letter.

I put my hand in the desk drawer and touched it every ten minutes. My heart beat fast and I smiled inside, knowing the letter was still there.

The first time I met you, I knew you were the one I was waiting for. You are so talented, beautiful, and kind. I am such a humble boy, but would you give me a chance to be with you? I would do whatever I could to catch up with you... He also told me what he liked about me and about our attending the same university one day. The letter made me feel special, and made the young deer dance around my stomach.

When I turned my head, I could see out of the corner of my own eye the pair of eyes looking at me. But I was too shy to look back at him. The letter was from Yang, a boy seated in the back row. His black-framed glasses made him appear more sophisticated than others our age. He was an excellent table-tennis player and a big fan of traditional Chinese literature.

He often came to talk to my friends and me during break time. And though our seats in the classroom were assigned—I sat in the first row—when we did experiments in the laboratory our seats were open, and he would always find a reason to sit near me. He said I reminded him of the girls in classical novels. I laughed loudly to cover my embarrassment. I was too shy to ask him what he meant.

I had the feeling there was going to be something more between us. I expected it and was eager to experience what love was like. But when I received the letter, I hesitated. The fear of disappointing my parents and teachers appeared in full-on sweaty guilt. *Should I reply to him? What should I say? Has Teacher Yun heard anything about this?* My head was swimming with questions. I could not concentrate on my homework.

If I accepted and then regretted it later, would I hurt him more than if I just turned him down now? If I started my first relationship purely out of curiosity, was I being selfish? I liked Yang, but it was too early to tell if we had a future. But did it matter? Even more, the biggest problem was that I just didn't have Wen's courage to withstand the humiliation from my teachers, headmaster, and parents.

The schoolyard that evening seemed to be more romantic than usual. Students relaxed between the dinner and evening study sessions. It had just rained. Yellowish paulownia leaves dropped on the gray bricks, paving the yard. Broken red begonia petals, glistening with rainwater, set off the greenery of the leaves. I closed my eyes and immersed myself in the smell of newly mowed grass. Pink and purple clouds were slowly settling at the horizon.

Students stuck to groups of four or five, some sitting on the steps in front of the school, listening to the latest pop songs from Taiwan, others standing under the paulownia tree chatting about the NBA games. It was obvious who had a crush on whom. The boy who hadn't ever yet had to shave was uneasy talking to the girl who had a nice pair of dimples. The bossiest girl with thick bangs unconsciously spoke gently each time our class monitor was around.

I retreated to the classroom and wrote a letter to Yang. I told him I wasn't ready for a relationship. *If I made you misunderstand me, I am very sorry. But I sincerely hope we can be good friends.*

He didn't give up.

In the second letter, he said he understood, and that he could wait until we went to university.

I replied that I didn't want to keep him waiting, and couldn't guarantee that I would like him then.

Yang changed his approach.

In his next letters, he asked my opinions on music and literature, which I was comfortable discussing more than relationships. Sometimes, he'd write a poem and ask for my ideas on how to improve it. I dropped my guard and was happy to give him my edits.

Our relationship began to exist in a sweet spot between friends and lovers.

We were both fond of writing letters. We talked about our plans for the future. He said his dream was to study Chinese literature at Peking University. *The water in Weiming Lake would flush away any troubles in life,* he wrote.

Most of the time, we exchanged letters during the evening self-study session. He would invite me to watch him play basketball. His slam dunks earned him a lot of attention from the girls.

It was fun, but then I sensed something was wrong. Not with him but with Teacher Yun. I didn't know if I was being paranoid, but I read something different in Teacher Yun's always-sharp eyes when they landed on me.

A fifteen-inch LED sign hung on the front wall of our classroom. The red characters—"365 days left before *gaokao*"—were bright and planted in the center, as if the teachers were afraid we'd forget the test's importance. The number changed automatically, counting down every day.

Every student had a hill of books covering half their desk. In the three rows, fifty of us sat facing the same direction. My head was covered behind my books as I did my work, and I could only hear the rustles of pens streaking across papers.

Teacher Yun rushed into our evening self-study session one day, holding in her right hand a stack of math test results. She glanced quickly around, her red-hot eyes landing over my book hill and giving me a chill. I looked down, but could still feel her eyes poking me.

She announced that my and ten other students' scores were very low.

"Listen up, I have to remind some of you of something," she added in a raised voice. "I know all about what you've been up to. I know your little tricks. Don't play with fire in my class. Love? How can you play such games when you don't even know how to keep your messy grades up? Respect yourselves! Otherwise, you're not welcome here. If you dare to step out of line, watch out, I have ways of teaching you a lesson."

I put my face down. Her words might not have been aimed at me, but a deep shiver shook my spine. I reached my hands into my drawer to find the letter I had just received from Yang, and buried it deep between the pages of a thick dictionary.

Yang waited for me outside the classroom that night when everybody else had left, but I walked away with a girl and pretended not to notice him. He sent me more letters, but I replied less and less frequently. When the next semester started, thankfully, he was moved to another class. We kept in touch, but I gave up on the idea of love entirely.

In the last letter I wrote to him, I said I wasn't brave enough to face the humiliation from Teacher Yun and, more importantly, I couldn't let my parents down. I disliked the rules and the *gaokao*, but I believed in the importance of sacrifice for the sake of a brighter future. In China, studying hard is just a means to reaching the next level. Education is a tool to weed out the unqualified and select the elite. I didn't want to be weeded out.

CHAPTER NINE

Red Silk Shoes
and a White Dress

Three years of high school passed quickly. In the summer of 2008, I received a letter of admission from Beijing International Studies University, a school that focused on foreign languages and culture. I had two months off before going to Beijing in late August.

That same summer, Chunting finished her first three years of vocational school and was excited to prepare for another two years of college at a campus in the Tianjin city center.

But Uncle Lishui had changed his mind.

If Chunting quit now, she could immediately get a graduation certificate and the school would find her a job, as promised in the pamphlet. Uncle Lishui calculated that if his daughter continued for two more years, he would have to spend another 20,000 yuan to cover tuition and living expenses, yet it wouldn't guarantee a white-collar job. Especially when it had become difficult for graduates of four-year universities to find decent work. He advised

Chunting to take a factory job that her school offered and look for a good husband.

Chunting did as she was told. She packed her bags, stood at the school gate for one last photo with her roommates, and then walked to the bus station. On the bus, she messaged her first boyfriend, Jiaming, asking what decision he had made for the next year. He said he was going to Tianjin for college. She wanted to text him: *Do we still have a chance?* but replaced it with a smiley face. She knew they didn't.

The school assigned Chunting an internship in a local factory producing pumping units used for drilling oil. Fifty people, from the age of eighteen to twenty-four—half of them from the vocational high school—stood in three lines at the factory entrance, ready for their six-month apprenticeship. Chunting and two other girls were picked to be a team. Their *shifu*, or supervisor, Chen, was a man in his early thirties whose face was covered with stubble.

Each *shifu* led his new apprentices to a room in a small building separated from the main workshop. A woman whose hair wasn't covered with a blue cap like the others gave them their uniforms: a loose blue cotton jacket and trousers, and a blue cap.

Chen sat down, lit a cigarette, and chatted with the women. Chunting noticed that black machine oil covered both of his hands, and that his fingers were hard and knobby, with skin far too worn and torn for a man his age. Through the room's small windows, she saw gray smoke belching so heavily from a chimney that it blurred the trees. This was not what she had imagined her job would look like, especially not when compared to the pages of a fashion magazine.

Chunting showed me photos she had taken of the place, using a new cell phone her father had given to her as a graduation gift. The factory compound was made up of a row of red-brick buildings, many stories high. Inside, vast machines used for different processes arranged for melting steel, pouring it into molds, polishing the finished product, and measuring their weight and size. Fifty or sixty people worked on each floor. Orders from domestic and international companies were heaped haphazardly in her manager's in-tray. Demand had increased in recent years and the factory now had three thousand workers.

Chunting worked from 8 a.m. to 7 p.m., with an hour's break for lunch. There were no weekends off. When there were too many orders, they had to work night shifts to make sure the machines ran twenty-four hours a day, seven days a week.

As an entry-level employee, Chunting was given the easiest job: in quality control. Chen *shifu* taught her how to measure the components, which had to be accurate down to the nearest 0.01 centimeter. She had to use her fingers to touch the surface of the products to feel for any damage or holes. The loud, growling machines, along with often-tight deadlines, made it impossible to ask questions. Chen *shifu* would shout into Chunting's ears whenever he needed to explain something.

The experienced workers earned 2,000 to 3,000 yuan per month at a time when the rent for a two-bedroom apartment in town cost around 800 yuan per month. As an apprentice, Chunting earned a monthly wage of only 500 yuan minus the lunch served at the canteen, which cost three yuan per day and which was deducted before they received their paychecks. The factory also offered health insurance and the opportunity to join a pension, which many workers declined because it would mean another 150 yuan deduction each month. Still, accidents happened, like when a woman's hair got caught in the machine, and she almost had her head taken off.

Chunting had never worked so hard. When she had lived with her parents, they looked after her, especially her mother, who did all the cooking and cleaning, including washing Chunting's clothes, even her underwear!

Within a few weeks, before receiving her first paycheck, Chunting decided to quit.

A friend had told her about a job at a wholesale shopping market. She needed to be there only to check the goods loaded in the van against the customers' orders, log items and their amount in a notebook, and operate the cash register. The salary was more than she was earning at the factory, and the work easier.

But when Chunting started the new job, she found it wasn't so easy. There were more than twenty kinds of soft drinks and two hundred types of snacks in the food section. In the daily necessities section, shampoos, soaps, and detergents of different brands sat haphazardly on the shelves without the prices being listed. Chunting had to memorize the price for each item and the discounts, which varied. Her boss handed Chunting a price list on her first day, but the drivers rushed her through it. "Quick, quick," they would say, and she spent the whole day flustered. If she counted the money or calculated the discounts incorrectly, her manager would deduct the missing sum from her already humble paycheck. If Chunting accidentally charged more, he never said a word.

Chunting's life had become a grind. The weekends I visited, she was so exhausted she only briefly said hello to us before going to her bedroom to sleep. If I asked about her job, the only thing she would say was: "It's boring."

It wasn't until she received her first paycheck that the light returned to Chunting's eyes. I was there when she finished work that evening. She took a shower, tied her fluffy hair into a ponytail, and put on rosy red lipstick.

"Let's go eat out," she said, nearly pulling me out the door. "I'll treat you!"

I was still on my summer break before the first semester of college. After the *gaokao* and my acceptance to a university, a weight had been lifted off my shoulders. For the first time in my life, I no longer needed to worry about anything related to school. I spent my days reading, watching movies, learning watercolor painting and guitar, all the useless things that students were discouraged to do before the *gaokao*.

Chunting and I went to KFC.

"I'm older than you, Miss Chunting, but you are the one making money first," I teased, sipping my Coke. "I'm so happy for you."

She smiled. "This is nothing. I only got 1,000 yuan this month. My boss is so stingy. She earns thousands every month, and treats us like her slaves," she said, grimacing. "Well, let's stop talking about that female *píxiū*. I have more exciting news."

I laughed. A *píxiū* was a creature in ancient Chinese legends who ate but never excreted.

"What?" I asked.

"I might be seeing someone..." Chunting blinked her big eyes.

"I knew it! You always hide in your room with your phone! I knew it!" I giggled.

Chunting's new boyfriend, Ling, was a driver in the market where she worked. He was three years older than us and had been chasing her.

"Maybe I won't date him," she said. "He's so tan, and I like guys with fair skin. His eyebrows are so thick that they almost connect."

We laughed.

"He's not as good-looking as I would want my boyfriend to be."

She looked like the little girl who used to lie in bed with me, talking about being an actress.

"More importantly," she continued, "I know my parents won't like it. His dad's not well."

"Ah," I said. "What's wrong with him?"

"He has lung cancer." Chunting sighed, looked away, and took a long sip of her Coke.

Since Chunting was no longer a student, there was no need to hide her relationships anymore. We had relatives in Ling's home village, Houmi, which was only a twenty-minute drive away. Everyone there knew his family had spent a lot of money trying to heal his father's cancer and that they were in debt. Ling's mother had taken over the farming. Ling was hardworking, but what future would a driver from a low-income family have? In those days, almost all girls asked their fiancé's family to buy an apartment in town after marriage, but Ling's parents couldn't afford it.

Three years earlier, Ling's parents had renovated their house in preparation for Ling's future bride, but no girl would agree to a second date when they learned there was no possibility of an apartment in town. Chunting was right. Once her parents heard of it, they and everyone else in our family would say she shouldn't see him.

I was unsure about what to think.

Chunting knew we all wanted what was best for her, but she found it difficult to stop hanging out with Ling, partly because they worked together. She made up her mind to break up with him, but within a week she missed him too much.

Gradually, her job became easier, and she was happy to see Ling every day. Before he drove back to the market to reload his van, he would send a message to Chunting so that she could prepare the order. When he arrived, the two would chat and enjoyed each other's company, mainly laughing about the crazy customers. After work, he would drive her to KFC or the new shopping center, New Century Capital. Chunting loved their dates to Uegashima Coffee, the first coffee shop in town. It sounded Japanese but was Chinese-owned. Neither Chunting nor Ling liked coffee, but there were other drinks on the menu. And the shop seemed so modern, with leather sofas, orange-tinted soft lighting, and the feeling of newness. Altogether it added a special atmosphere to their dates.

Beijing was hosting the summer Olympic Games that year. For months, the city had been in a frenzy of activity in preparation, with many ultra-modern new buildings constructed to complement the new stadiums and show off the new, emerging China to the rest of the world. I was glued to the TV, cheering for our athletes, but Chunting was not interested at all. Her whole focus was on love. She seemed to check her phone every minute, smiling while reading the messages from Ling, and seemed far away during our conversations. After dinner, she would immediately lock herself in the room we shared while I'd sit chatting with our parents. I envied her. It looked nice to be in love. She was glowing and it made me daydream about what sort of boyfriend I'd like to have. *Would I like a man like Ling?* Probably not. I imagined my boyfriend to be a writer, a musician, or a professor, someone who would love the poems I'd write him. And he'd be someone who lived in the urban, sophisticated atmosphere of the city. Those were my fantasies.

Chunting was only nineteen years old and just having fun, but their families, especially Ling's, didn't think so. Ling was twenty-two, still very young, but in the village, competition to find a wife was fierce. The gender ratio for the marriageable population in China is strikingly imbalanced as a consequence of the One-Child Policy and the preference for boys. A poor villager's chance of finding a wife was slim. The unfortunate single men—villagers or not—were called *guānggùn*, or "bachelors," like a tree branch that bore no leaves or fruit.

China had never in its history had such a big *guānggùn* population.

During the thirty-year One-Child Policy, families had thrown many girls away, drowning, smothering, or aborting them. Scholars believe that 30 to 60 million girls "disappeared" due to the One-Child Policy.

The tables had turned and, given that women could now be selective (despite playing hard to get), they tended to marry men with better economic backgrounds. Village girls tended to marry town boys, and town girls to marry city boys, leaving the rural boys wanting.

Some families used marriage agents or matchmakers to introduce girls from the poorest areas like Inner Mongolia to the rural men in our village. Some families were so desperate they paid agents to find girls from neighboring countries like Vietnam or North Korea, especially defectors. Many such brides entered China without any legal paperwork, and it was common to hear about such "mail-order brides"—many of them trafficked and there against their own free will—who would run away shortly after marriage.

In Ling's village, with a population of 1,500, there were more than twenty *guānggùn*. Some of them in their thirties. So with Chunting on the scene, Ling's parents didn't want to lose their chance. They sent a matchmaker to Uncle Lishui's door to propose marriage. Although it had by then become common for young people to marry for love, to show their respect, the man's family still asked for help from a matchmaker to negotiate the marriage details with the woman's family.

Matchmakers are usually married women who know both families. It's not a full-time job, but, in Chinese culture, if you have successfully matched a couple, it is believed you will be blessed with good karma. To show their gratitude, the man's family gives gifts to matchmakers too. When my parents married in the 1980s, the gift was twenty chicken eggs and a bag of rice. Today, the gift is always a lucky red envelope filled with crisp new yuans, from a few hundred to a few thousand.

"Ling's parents really like Chunting, and as you can see, the two children are a well-suited match," said the matchmaker, a fortysomething woman married to a Caiyuan villager.

Uncle Lishui smiled and offered her a plate of fruit. Even when you refuse a marriage proposal, it is important to save "face"—that is, maintain a semblance of your own and, sometimes more importantly, the other person's self-respect.

"I understand how decent Ling's parents are, and how hardworking he is, but Chunting is still young; we don't want to be rushed."

In fact, many marriage proposals were waiting for Chunting. After a girl left school, all eyes were fixed on her. Suddenly she was a hot commodity. Among Chunting's suitors, most were from Lutai, and a few from Tianjin. But Chunting turned them all down, saying she couldn't meet them while she was in a relationship with Ling. My family thought she was crazy. Chunting still had a few years to decide, but needed to be more practical. After twenty-five, her "season" would be over.

"I understand, but here's my concern," said the matchmaker. "She'll be the one to lose out if she keeps hanging around with Ling. A man doesn't worry about rumors; a good man can wait a long time, and still many women will want to marry him. Girls cannot afford such luxury."

She played her cards nicely, and exchanged a few cordial rounds back and forth with Uncle Lishui. A good matchmaker, she said many nice things about Ling and his family, including the fact that Ling's father was on a diet of "special ingredients" prescribed by an experienced and highly respected traditional-medicine doctor whose fees were less than those charged by a doctor practicing Western-style medicine. In short, this meant his illness wouldn't cost the family as much as had been feared or rumored.

I encouraged Chunting to stick with Ling if she loved him. She should be the one who had the final say, not their parents. She had a whole life in front of her. She was not her parents' puppy or possession. Uncle Lishui said I read too many romantic books, and this was real life; money and a family's background mattered.

I again thought about the difficulties my parents had gone through in moving from the village to Lutai. If my mom had married somebody from Lutai with an urban *hukou* and a lot of money, her life would have been much more comfortable. Though I felt I'd have to marry for love—or else I wouldn't be able to live with myself—maybe our parents were right. Chunting faced a big dilemma.

She decided to quit her job, this time to lessen her contact with Ling. To further break up the young couple, our family started to arrange blind dates with "suitable" candidates; that is, only when both sides were clear on basic information about each other were they allowed to meet. The information included their age, height, and education, as well as their parents' ages, and whether they had siblings who still needed support.

It was still tough, because all the suitors' information would be glorified by the matchmakers—a plain-faced man was described as "very handsome," his parents always "good tempered" and "good at saving money." The language of the matchmakers was carefully coded.

In the first meeting, the parents would take their children to the matchmaker's house, leaving the two young people alone to chat, the parents and matchmaker talking in another room.

Chunting had a few blind dates, none of them successful. The guys were either too shy or too chatty. Another young man was all right, but his parents were not satisfied with Chunting's height. He was only five-feet-five, and his parents wanted their son to marry a girl taller to "improve their genes." Chunting was only four-feet-nine.

All were involved in each step of the process. A blind date was the first step to marriage between adults, not a game between children.

*   *   *

A few weeks after the matchmaker visited in the early autumn, Chunting caught a cold that lasted an entire month.

Her face was pale and she threw up every morning. She also put on weight. One morning after breakfast, Chunting rushed to the yard and vomited. My mom and the other women in the house exchanged looks.

That afternoon, Mom asked Chunting if everything was okay. Chunting said she thought so, but wasn't sure. She hadn't had a period for two months.

She was given a pregnancy test.

I heard the news from Chunting herself, who spoke to me in her small room, her eyes swollen with tears. "They never taught me anything, and now they blame me for making mistakes," Chunting said. The ceiling fan helped circulate a little cool breeze from two windows, but I felt sluggish in the muggy air and with such a depressing situation. I suggested that she have an abortion, telling her she could go to a small clinic instead of a hospital to avoid being seen by people she knew.

Abortion advertisements were everywhere, on electricity poles, coffee-shop bathrooms, in the fish market. They promised a "painless, three-minute" surgery, no ID required. So even minors could do it without their parents' permission. At nineteen years old, I didn't realize what irresponsible advice I was giving her: Women died at these clinics, which were often unlicensed, or suffered from debilitating pain or fertility loss. All I knew was that Chunting was too young, and unmarried, and that I didn't want to lose my best friend. I was desperate to set my cousin free from the swamp she was sinking into.

Uncle Lishui and Aunt Zhirong were furious, but not shocked. It had become less rare to see accidental pregnancies before marriage. It would be better, though, if Chunting and Ling did marry, even if the pregnancy meant our family was now at a disadvantage in the bargaining.

When Ling's family found out, they sent the matchmaker back to Uncle Lishui.

The woman gave a quick but obvious glance at Chunting's belly. Chunting, who was sitting at the window, pretended she didn't notice. I sat next to her and listened to every word in the negotiation. In this same room, Chunting and I had talked so much of our rosy dreams, of being an actress, a singer, a professional woman who wore silk scarves around her neck to the office. We had dreamed about our future husbands: They would be tall, handsome gentlemen with warm smiles that we'd fall in love with. In our dream weddings, there wasn't a matchmaker in sight. This was all I could think about.

I saw Chunting's dream broken right in front of me. What would happen to me? We had grown up together, watched the same TV shows, had the same hairstyles, and shared the same friends; this could easily happen to me too. Laolao once had a fortune-teller predict my future. I forgot most of what he said, but remembered one thing: *She sets her ambition higher than the moon.* Was it a compliment or an omen? Chunting and I had started at the same point. How would I fare by comparison?

"Let's talk about *caili.*" Uncle Lishui finally hit on the main issue of the evening's bargaining. *Caili,* the bride price, was the main measure of a man's financial power and sincerity. "You know *caili* is a tradition. If we don't accept, it doesn't look good on either side, does it?"

"*Aiyaya*, of course Ling will give you *caili*, and I have told his parents that you are not the type who would ask for a lot of money. *Caili* can be tens of thousands of yuan or millions. I'm sure Chunting won't be happy in a marriage if her parents-in-law had to borrow so much for her *caili*, would she?"

In ancient times, the bridegroom's family gave the bride's family *caili* and a letter confirming the engagement, which worked as a contract and a proclamation of the woman's worth. The more money and gifts the woman received, the more her future husband and parents-in-law respected her—in theory. Paying money and gifts was also regarded as a way to thank the woman's parents for raising her well. If the woman quit the marriage, her family had to return the *caili*; if the man quit, he wouldn't get a penny back.

Mao's revolution introduced women to the workplace and reformed marriage law to ensure that women and men enjoyed equal status for the first time in Chinese history— at least on paper. The *caili* system was criticized by Mao as a form of gender discrimination. But *caili* never ended, especially in the countryside. An interesting phenomenon was that the poorer a region was, and the fewer the available women were, the higher the bar the local people set for *caili*. Although the government issued an administrative paper to curb *caili* from increasing, in reality it was a supply-and-demand dynamic.

When Chunting's marriage was being negotiated, an average *caili* was at least 70,000 yuan. In addition, the groom's family had to provide a house or apartment for the newlyweds. The price of housing started to soar in the early 2000s. A simple furnished two-bedroom apartment in Lutai was at least 500,000 yuan, equivalent to $78,000.

Families with daughters believed *caili* was one of the "now or never" chances of financial support. Women seldom complained about the system. People still believed that the more a man invested, the more stable the marriage would be. Not many families could afford a second marriage.

I informed my parents that I wouldn't ask for any *caili* when I got married, because I found it insulting. We were no longer living in the Qing dynasty, when a woman couldn't support herself and her family by her own means— unless she was an empress, of course. And why should a man pay a woman to marry him? To me, *caili* made women look weak.

But, clearly, with her pregnancy, Chunting lost in the bargain no matter how hard the families tried to pretend it would be a typical negotiation. Ling's family offered a relatively meager 50,000 yuan, which Uncle Lishui accepted.

I was not happy with any of it, the *caili* system or the marriage. Chunting was not a goat, and should not be sold! When we were young, she and I laughed at people who talked about *caili*. I urged her to think for herself, but I couldn't give any better suggestions. What did I know about marriage and children? My idealism was founded on nothing; I was only due to start college in August. Chunting didn't have an escape route. If they refused Ling's offer, it would mean Chunting would have to get an abortion. If she went this route, she might face the wrath of village gossip; rumors still spread quickly. Chunting's reputation could very possibly be badly damaged. If that happened, who would propose to her again? And what would her "price" be then?

On her wedding day, Chunting wore a white, Western-style dress instead of a traditional lucky-red dress, and sat beforehand with me in her parents' room. As we waited for Ling and his family to take her away, I kept my eyes down, on her shoes. As a nod to tradition, and a small concession to the wishes of Ling's parents, she wore red silk slippers, embroidered with plum branches in bloom and flying mag-pies to signify happiness.

Chunting touched her belly. She had put on more weight than she had expected to, at only four months pregnant. The dress was a bit tight. I adjusted the fresh red roses in her tied-up hair.

"You look beautiful," I said.

"This is it." Chunting gave me a wry smile. "I still can't believe it. I hope you can visit me a lot."

By about 10 a.m., Uncle Lishui's home was packed with people. Two golden characters for double happiness, or *xi*, printed on bright red paper, were hung by the front gate.

Chunting raised her eyes when the host explained the details of the ceremony: "Your husband will lift you up and take you to the car; you will hand out candy or cigarettes to all his relatives, along with red envelopes to their children, when they bless you..."

I held her hand, just as I had when we were little girls. When the host left, I asked if she still remembered that one afternoon when we were seven and had decided to run away from home after watching the cartoon *Haier Brothers*, with two little brothers who were always traveling. We had planned to do the same. We'd often walk far along the river—escaping. It felt as if we'd walk for hours, but Uncle Lishui always easily caught up to us and beckoned us to dinner. We had promised each other that one day, when we were grown up, we would go to faraway places, just like the Haier brothers.

"Of course I remember," said Chunting. "You're going to accomplish that soon. I'm not. You'll have to do it for both of us."

Chunting told me there were so many things she'd never done and probably would never do now, due to her sudden circumstance. Marriage was the best option she had, and she had to face it.

"Are you ready?" I forced a smile on my face. "They will come to take you away from me soon." I fetched her red velvet purse and helped her do a last check of her things: red envelopes, a small ring box wrapped in glittery red cloth, makeup, a red dress to change into for the toast at lunch, and the marriage certificate with her and Ling's photos.

Outside, fireworks were set alight, and there was much chatter and laughter. From the window, we watched as a black car pulled up to take her away and into the next chapter of her life.

CHAPTER TEN

Children of Tiananmen

Beijing, 2008

I t had been the most relaxing summer holiday of my life. Beijing had hosted the Olympic Games, the "most important event in a hundred years," said the media. For the first time, China topped the gold medals list.

We were becoming obsessed with *–ests*: China's plan to build the world's biggest shopping mall, to have the world's longest railway, our GDP growth as the world's fastest, the Great Wall was the world's largest. We'd had enough humiliation. The Olympics showed that China could do things as well as the West—or even better. China had become the third country to send humans into space, after Russia and the US, and had started work on building a space station and launching a manned expedition to the moon. China's economy had been expanding for decades, and would soon overtake Japan to become the world's second largest. China's first bullet train was launched, speeding between Beijing and Tianjin in only thirty minutes in a journey that had until then taken two hours. Folks stood in long lines for tickets just to experience a "bullet." They joked that the trip was so short, you'd waste the ticket if you had to use the bathroom. I left home with a small amount of luggage and an inflated sense of pride.

Before leaving for college, I met Chunting at Uncle Lishui's home. I didn't know what I would say. After her marriage, I hadn't seen much of her that summer. Things had changed quickly. We weren't the same schoolgirls on similar paths. The fork in our road grew rapidly wider.

She settled down in her husband's village and decided to rest for the remainder of the pregnancy. I was excited about the baby but nervous for her. I still didn't think she had made the right decision, and it almost killed me to look at her in this new life. Her eyes were droopy, and she couldn't fake enthusiasm in seeing me either. We just sat down next to each other, hand in hand. I wanted to tell her how excited I was about going to Beijing, about seeing the national flag-raising ceremony at Tiananmen Square like we had always planned, about spending the weekends at art exhibitions and meeting new friends from all over the country, or from all over the world. All my hard work for the *gaokao* had paid off. It was the bridge I was crossing to my future, and I wanted so badly to talk to Chunting about all the possibilities, but I couldn't. It would hurt her feelings. She was staying behind, with no clear plan beyond being a wife and mother.

Her head hung low as we sat together in her old room and she rubbed her stomach. I tried to cheer her up by telling her how happy she would be the next time I saw her, in six months when the baby was born.

"Will you still miss me after you have your fancy new friends?" she asked, forcing a small smile.

I felt a throb of pain in my throat, but put on a big smile. "Of course," I said, "I'll talk to you on the phone almost every day."

★   ★   ★

Since my parents knew nothing about Beijing or college life, Yunxiang offered to help me settle in. The next morning, we caught the 7 a.m. bus. My eyes were wide open, taking in every inch of the drive, while most other passengers napped.

As we left Lutai, I saw homes and shops turn into fields. Farmers dotted across the yellow paddy fields, their green and red headscarves bright in the early morning sun. We passed the field where Grandfather Wengui used to work. I remembered him resting on the ridge, smoking tobacco. We passed Caiyuan, and I remembered Laolao peeling the green beans on her *kang*. The bus also passed Chaoyang Village, where I was born. I recognized a few men I knew sitting at the village entrance. They had aged and seemed smaller, frailer, while I was taller and felt as if I could fly to the sky.

After an hour or so, the scenery was no longer familiar. There were woods, rivers, vineyards, and flocks of sheep in villages that seemed strange to me, reminding me of the feeling I had on my first trip to Beijing ten years earlier, when we visited Uncle Siyong. The clean, wide avenues, under the shade of paulownia trees, and the blue-and-white trolleys had fascinated me. The ticket sellers would pop their heads out the window and shout "Attention!" when the trolleys made a turn. There was so much more happening than in the familiar quietude of my village. I took a photo in front of the vast Tiananmen Square, Mao Zedong's portrait prominently displayed on the wall of the gate tower behind me.

After the photo, we saw a woman wearing an armband with a badge that read "Beijing Civilization Observer" stop a man who had just spit on the ground and fine him twenty yuan on the spot. He was shocked, and so were we. Spitting would never have been punished in our small town.

To my grandparents' generation, Beijing was a sacred city, former home to our past emperors and royal families. According to the old people, Beijing had the best feng shui, the best geomancy. *Yuhuangdadi*, or emperor of the heavens, had blessed the city. Beijing had not experienced any serious floods, no earthquakes or any natural disasters. Beijing was a holy city where all the important people lived: the Chinese Communist Party's top leaders, the army generals, and our greatest artists, scientists, engineers, and intellectuals—and their offspring.

Everyone in Caiyuan could point in Beijing's direction, but few had the chance to go there.

With the strict *hukou* system, before the 1980s, only when you had a reason approved by the government were you allowed to ride on the slow, green train to the capital. Laoye said that as a young farmer, no matter how tired he became, when he heard the radio announcers say in their polished Mandarin, "It's seven o'clock, Beijing time," he would feel a sense of hope; there would always be the dream of living in Beijing one day. When Uncle Siyong was transferred to his military unit in Beijing, Laolao knelt down in front of the ancestors' shrine and kowtowed to thank them for their blessing.

When my parents were young, all paintings and pictures decorating their walls were of the great capital city: children holding flowers and dancing in Tiananmen Square, pigeons flying over the blue sky at the Great Wall, and families rowing boats in Beihai Park. Beijing had the best of everything.

When the *hukou* restrictions loosened in 1980s, everyone could travel freely to Beijing for work if they wanted; however, they were reluctant to go, partly because of the prejudices they suffered for being migrant workers, without a city *hukou* and no permanent residence, therefore no stable job. But university students were different.

My neighbors and relatives believed it was a real achievement for me to go to Beijing to study. I was proud, too, but wondered where the capital would take me.

At 9:30 a.m., we arrived at the central bus station. The city looked even more like what I had seen on television than it did ten years before: skyscrapers and flashing billboards, heavy traffic, working women in smart suits holding disposable cups of soy milk as they walked to work, traffic policemen pointing cars here and there. The din was so loud it was as if ten video games were on at the same time, with honking car horns, bicycle bells, men in white shirts and black ties chatting loudly into their phones, street artists singing, and the drilling and hammering vibrations of construction. I loved it all, even the noise.

After a short subway ride, Yunxiang and I arrived at Beijing International Studies University, or BISU. Evergreens and pine trees, peonies and roses, were bathed in sunshine. All the buildings were painted either gray or dark orange, which made the small campus look tidy and clean. There was a big library and a new athletic center with an Olympic-size swimming pool.

When we arrived at the dorm, we found a lot of people in my room—mainly the families of my roommates, including Yun. Pretty and energetic, she had just dyed her hair brown and was learning jazz dance. We had been assigned bunks, and hers was below mine. My other roommate, Tian, a small girl with bangs cut to make her look like a traditional Japanese doll, liked Japanese animation and manga. She looked so young, I would have guessed she was no older than fourteen. Qi was the mysterious and elegant one. She didn't talk much, but smiled a lot. Na was easygoing—and was from Beijing's suburbs. Mei was a full-figured girl with short hair and thick glasses and tended to wear simple clothes: white or gray T-shirts, sporty trousers and shoes. Not long after we moved in together, I heard Mei was a lesbian and had a girlfriend in the Korean language department.

I asked Yunxiang if we could go for a walk. For some reason, I wasn't ready to be left alone.

The campus was full of activity. Parents hauled luggage, school coordinators held welcome banners, groups of girls chatted on their way to the shower house, boys ran to the basketball courts. And there were wandering magpies everywhere—I remember feeling as lost as they seemed to be.

Before he left, Yunxiang handed me some cash to buy things I needed, like soap and shampoo.

"Listen, Chaoqun, here's some advice: Don't fight with girls in your dorm, don't eat the street food, don't get back to the dorm late, and call me whenever you need to."

I felt like he was nervous, which made me more nervous. I could barely focus on what he was saying.

But the moment I watched him walk away, I stood in the dorm lobby, and suddenly felt a huge rush of adrenaline. *I made it!* I wanted to cheer. *Yesss!* I had been ready to be a grown-up for too long. The time had finally arrived, and my dream was happening right now, right in front of me. I was standing in my dream. It was my first time living far away from my parents, my first time sharing a room with people I didn't know at all, and my first time deciding how to spend my money and my time. I was like a newly grown cat, poised, ready to pounce on her prey, though a little uncertain that she had acquired the necessary skills.

The first two weeks of university life were filled with meetings: with teachers, organized academic departments, and student union leaders; meetings to choose which clubs to join; meetings about how to use the student ID card to get water, take showers, buy food, and use the library; and, most importantly, meetings with our *fŭdăoyuán*, my political counselor-adviser, Guan Xin.

A *fǔdǎoyuán* is appointed to each grade. They help students academically and professionally, organize activities, and monitor the students' mental health, but their most important duty is to provide political instruction and build unity between students and the party. Guan Xin was only five or six years older than me. He had just finished his master's program at a university in Northeast China. He wore thick glasses, kept his hair short and neat, and seemed to have an endless supply of checkered shirts. He was plump and walked like a penguin, which took me a while to stop giggling about.

He had to supervise three hundred of us, and was expected to know us so well that he could predict if we were suicidal, murderous, or revolutionary.

Two weeks after my arrival, Guan Xin said I had to start *junxun*, a form of military training all college freshmen in China must complete. It was supposed to give us a tougher mind-set. *Junxun* lasted anywhere from two weeks to a month. It had been expanded and more formalized after the Tiananmen Square incident on June 4, when the government sent soldiers to clear people out from the square, during which many students were killed.

Discussion of the June Fourth Incident was prohibited. I was curious about the movement, but our generation had no way of learning more, despite living with the consequences of it.

A few sophomore girls gave my roommates and me some notes to prepare us for *junxun*: Pack sunscreen, don't take fruits or snacks, just listen, don't ask questions. The worst part to me was that we could not take our phones. I panicked, thinking: *How will I survive without my phone for two weeks?* Yunxiang had bought me a pink Nokia 6120 and I texted my friends back home every day.

Junxun sounded ridiculous, to say the least. *How is this boot camp supposed to make me love the government and appreciate the party more?* I was sure I hated the idea before it even started.

Tian had her parents use their connections to get her a letter from the local hospital stating that she had just had serious surgery on her leg and couldn't go. Guan Xin accepted the letter but told Tian she would have to complete the training next year if she wanted to graduate.

We were bused to a military base in Changping, a suburban district one and a half hours north of Beijing. We arrived at what seemed to be the middle of nowhere, in a forest of poplar trees and dark green mountains in the distance, and parked in front of a small compound. Hanging on the front wall was a large red banner: "Welcome, Soldiers from Beijing International Studies University."

We got off the bus and walked through the front gate and found ourselves in a time warp, as if we were in a TV drama from the 1970s. The building itself was four or five stories high, cream-colored and without any external decoration except for the banner. A man wearing fatigues waved his hand and directed us to follow him to a yard, where the welcoming ceremony would be held. The university's president and each department's director had already arrived and were standing on a stage set up in front of us.

The ceremony started with the raising of the national flag to the music of the national anthem. Our president and the director of the military base gave speeches but I hardly paid attention. My mind was consumed by the twenty or so uniformed men and women who stood beside the stage—I wondered what their roles would be.

We were divided into thirty groups, with men and women separate. I was put in team fourteen, with another forty girls. The *jiaoguan*, or drill instructors, went around to locate their teams. Our *jiaoguan*, Liu Lihu, had a round baby face. We were told to address him as "Sir Liu." He had been a real soldier and had just finished his two years of service.

Sir Liu took us to a room where we were given a set of uniforms, which did not look as crisp as the instructors'. My pants had been washed so many times that the green camouflage had faded into an almost pale white. The fabric was so thin and worn it looked as if the clothes would disintegrate. The zipper on my pants was broken, so I had to use safety pins to keep them closed. And they were so ill-fitting, even the smallest shirt was too big for me and many of the other girls.

It was September but Beijing was still boiling hot. The burning sun scorched the earth yellow and heat radiated off the pebbles. I was sweating before the training even began.

Our dormitory did not have air-conditioning or fans. The bunk beds were hard, and the quilts filthy with stains. I decided to sleep with my clothes on. Liu warned us that at any moment he might blow the whistle and we'd have five minutes to get dressed and gather into formation outside. We needed to be ready at all times, for anything, he said.

Mosquitoes buzzed at night. It felt as if they were

swarming our dormitory by the millions. I'd look like a
pepperoni pizza in the morning from all the bites.

We got up at 5:30 a.m. and went to bed at 10 p.m. In
the morning, we'd run for thirty minutes and then do thirty
minutes of *junlvquan*, or stretching. We were taught to
march in military two-steps, moving our legs in unison
upon the *jiaoguan*'s instruction, "one-two-one." One was
left foot, and two was right foot.

We had the same breakfast every day: rice porridge, pickled cabbage, seaweed and peanuts, spicy and salty tofu, and
a boiled egg, and had to stand, ten students to a table, to eat.
If we weren't quiet enough while we waited to be served,
a *jiaoguan* could make us squat under the table until the
others finished eating. No one was allowed to touch their
chopsticks without the *jiaoguan*'s permission. For lunch
and dinner, the formation that marched the most sharply
in unison and chanted the patriotic marching songs the
loudest was allowed into the canteen first. If our *jiaoguan*
believed we were not trying hard enough, he would delay
mealtime. No one wanted that. After a day filled with activities of all sorts, by dinner, it felt as if my stomach had
been buried in my back. When the *jiaoguan* blew his whistle to signal that we could begin eating, we went at our food
like a pack of hungry wolves. There were only four com-
munal dishes placed before us, to be shared. For the first
few meals, I was polite and ate at my usual speed. One day
a girl standing next to me started scooping more than her
share into her own bowl, and it became a full-on scram-
ble. I wasn't quick enough to get much beyond the only
things left: dry and tasteless rice and steamed buns. From

that day on, I forgot about being polite. Before the *jiaoguan* blew his whistle, I would already have my eyes fixed on the dish I wanted and had strategized the right angle to stretch out my chopsticks. When I heard the whistle, I'd jump up and grab as much as I could manage to hoard. Within one minute, the dishes were empty; we all ate silently, holding our bowls close.

Everything in training was about being straight. We had to stand up straight, sit up straight, and speak facing straight forward. Before we could go to the toilet or drink a swig of water, we had to ask permission. We were taught that obedience is the first principle for good soldiers, even temporary soldiers like us.

On the first day, we had to hand in our phones, but some girls hid theirs inside their extra shoes or in their pillows.

One night, a girl typed messages under her quilt with the sound on loud enough for us all to hear. She didn't know Liu was walking outside our window. Suddenly he blew hard on his whistle. I nearly jumped out of bed. When we had assembled, standing to attention, Sir Liu demanded that we hand in any hidden phones or else we wouldn't be sleeping that night. I tried not to eye the girls who still had their phones, and I could see that many other girls were just as angry as I was. All I wanted to do was sleep. My muscles ached from a long march we had gone on earlier, and I felt dehydrated. It was already midnight and we had to be back up in five hours. I wanted to scream!

Then, suddenly, three girls gave up their phones.

When I placed my head back on the hard bunk, it was the happiest I'd been since our arrival.

After the day's training, the students took turns shower-ing. Team one went first. In the women's bathroom, about thirty taps were installed, one next to another and without any dividing curtains or stalls. By the time it was my turn, the hot water had all been used. I stood naked, shivering, turning my body to face the wall. But I had no time to complain. The officers gave us only fifteen minutes, and this included getting undressed, dressed, and making sure everything was tidy when we were done. Punishment for being late would be thirty push-ups.

I didn't understand the *jiaoguans'* agenda or their rules. We were not soldiers. Yet every morning we had two hours of "military theory lessons" in the canteen. The dining ta-bles were moved to a corner, and we sat on the floor. A wooden desk was put in the middle of the room for guest speakers from the Party School of the Central Committee, who droned on and on in an almost robotic fashion about Chinese military defense systems, wars, and geopolitics. Most of us ended up falling asleep during their lectures.

In the first few days, Sir Liu would yell at the napping students and take them out to stand in the sun as punish-ment, but soon this stopped being effective. There were too many napping students, and he couldn't keep interrupting the guest speaker.

Some speakers read the materials plainly and left, but others relished the opportunity to teach us young spoiled kids a real lesson.

Years ago, when politics was thrust upon me in school, I felt a need to respect it enough to try to care. I wanted to know what I should think and desire, and I was grateful to have the government there to tell me. My friends and classmates felt the same, but growing up with a mothering government all your life, there is only one thing to do: grow tired of it. I was not interested in learning how to be a Chinese soldier, and I was growing annoyed with being their student. When you are forced to love something, it loses all its charm.

"Do you know why this class is important?" one speaker, Professor Chen, asked.

Professor Chen looked fiftysomething and had a thin, solemn face. His voice was resonant and deep, and he sat very straight. He was decorated with more medals than any other speaker. "You think the idea of war is far off, don't you?" He paused for a few seconds. "No! We're very close to war—more than you think. There is a global bully—called the USA—and don't you forget it!"

A few of us looked at each other, wondering where the heck he was going with this.

"Since the collapse of the Soviet Union, the US has never dropped its ambitions to overthrow our party and cause unrest in our country. The US peddles its values all over the world and goes to war with any country who won't listen. Americans engage in spiritual colonization and call it 'American culture.'" He sneered. "You need to watch out, every one of you." He shouted his last plea at a high volume: "Watch out!"

Though the fans rotated hypnotically and the windows were open, inside it felt like a steamer. It didn't help that we had someone yelling at us. I longed to call someone at home to come and get me.

"We should be alert," continued Professor Chen. "Americans believe that only their system is *real* democracy. Eastern European countries once believed that if they had democracy, they would have everything. It was a lie! Abandoning socialism has weakened them. Nobody respects a weak and poor country, no matter what political system it has. Remember that."

I was so drowsy I just wanted his speech to end, but he went on. "Corruption is not a product of the socialist system. Russia has a so-called elected president, but corruption is still rampant. India has a democracy, but it's all chaos. Don't be naive like those students in 1989 who believed Western democracy would bring about a perfect world."

Suddenly I perked up, surprised that he mentioned the 1989 incident. Now I wanted him to say more. "Lies!" he said, but didn't elaborate.

I had heard people refer to the 1989 protest and the June Fourth Tiananmen Massacre; as I mentioned earlier, the protest lasted for more than a month but what makes June Fourth so memorable are the killings.

Although subjects like the Cultural Revolution and the Great Leap Forward were still sensitive, people were relatively eager to talk about them. The 1989 student riot seemed to be the most sensitive story, because my family just shrugged away any questions I had about it.

"You are the generation of 1989," a family friend once said to me. I wanted him to go on, but he didn't. "You'll understand when you get older."

One day, when I was about twelve, I found a copy of *Banyuetan* magazine that explained it:

In the late 1980s, the liberals, bewitched by Western ideology, promoted the propaganda of Western democracy, and they plotted to subvert the government and socialist system and overthrow the Chinese Communist Party. The liberals took advantage of university students and their dissatisfaction with domestic problems and instigated them to protest in Tiananmen Square. Riots and crimes such as robbery, arson, and vandalism occurred in Beijing and other major cities. To maintain stability and protect the people, the government summoned the army to Beijing to quiet down the riot.

That was all I knew.

But as I've grown older, I realize my personal connection with 1989 goes far beyond just the year I was born. Lying in my bunk bed in the Changping military base, I realized that I was no longer a typical Chinese student. I wanted more than to be told when to pee, what to drink, and when to feel that I wanted social change.

During high school, in a class called the Comprehensive History of Modern and Contemporary China, I looked for a chapter in our textbook and on the syllabus about 1989, but there was no mention of it. Normally, I would not have expected to see it, but our teacher, Teacher Xioping, was different from the others. She was in her forties and wore vintage, floral-patterned dresses. On the first day, she wrote on the blackboard, *Never blindly believe in anything told by your teacher.* In her class, she always threw questions in the air; it wasn't just about memorization. Her bright eyes were full of expectation. She didn't ask us to raise our hands. We could talk or even shout out the answers if we liked. She didn't want robots in her class; she wanted us to learn and study with our whole mind and, more importantly, our hearts. She challenged us to look for answers.

When I told her that the history textbook was missing the year of my birth, she said, "It could never be explained fairly in a Chinese textbook, Chaoqun."

I was disappointed.

She continued: "A Chinese textbook could never illustrate the vibrancy of the 1980s. Don't rely too closely on these books. When you get older, try to read as much as possible, and find the truth of right and wrong for yourself."

Teacher Xioping was unlike any teacher I had ever met. She spoke to us of dreams, philosophy, art, and poems— and it wasn't just the patriotic propaganda. There was an eagerness in her eyes to tell us more, to inspire us, but still, she was like a dancer in chains. She was reluctant to explain too much. She'd get in trouble.

Few of my classmates and friends were curious about June Fourth or admired Teacher Xioping as I did. Questioning was not valued, so the students didn't bother. Our parents and instructors taught us for years that too much curiosity would bring us trouble. Change was downplayed and criticized, and seemed to be inappropriate for the era we lived in. My generation was already lucky—we had modern products and entertainment to distract us—to pacify us into submission. But I longed for 1989, and filled my days with dreams of what it would be like to challenge, to be vocal, and to change things.

The rest of the *junxun* passed much faster. During the closing ceremony, the university president and each department's director spoke onstage again. They were in uniform, but this time so was I. I marched past the stage in lockstep and chanted in unison like a little soldier: "Study hard and protect the motherland." It was our graduation. We were taught to obey and accept orders, and to enjoy it, to think about nothing and make no decisions for ourselves, just follow and obey... Except, in my heart, I had already made a decision not to.

★   ★   ★

When my classmates and I returned to normal life, things were pretty much the same. We again spent too much time on our phones, and slept in late. We still complained about the food in the canteens. But military training had left some mark on us. I wondered how different it had made me. If college students were as blank as a sheet of clean paper, the *junxun* was the first color we were painted. Even if it faded with time, it would always be there, part of us.

The most blatant mark *junxun* left on me was that I was now determined to discover the truth about June Fourth.

CHAPTER ELEVEN

A Cocktail Bar in Beijing

I could smell love everywhere on campus. In front of our dormitory was a rose garden. When I finished my evening classes, walking back to my room, I always came across couples on dates there, kissing and whispering to each other. I would turn my head away to avoid embarrassing them, but secretly I enjoyed seeing it.

Love, I'd think, turned people into conjoined babies: They ate together, studied together, walked together holding hands. Seeing how happy these couples were, I felt lonely, and left out. It had only been three months since I had graduated from high school, but most girls my age had boyfriends.

There was a lounge in the girls' dorms, and it was always full of guys waiting for their girlfriends. Among my six roommates, only Na, the girl from the suburbs, had a stable relationship with her high school sweetheart. Yun was the most popular, and changed boyfriends every week. She said it was not her fault; even when she was studying in the library, boys she didn't know would walk up to her and ask for her phone number.

I was most fascinated by Mei's relationship with a woman. I had never met a lesbian. In Lutai, people called lesbian and gay people perverts, and in our schoolbooks, homosexuality was described as a mental illness.

At the university, many people were honest about their sexuality, and I never heard anybody speaking badly about homosexuality, but Mei never talked to us about her relationship. Once I saw her crying in her bed, and I heard from Na that Mei's girlfriend had suddenly announced she was in love with a man. She was bisexual and Mei couldn't accept it.

I did have a few guys interested in me. Yang, the boy who chased me in high school, kept writing love letters to me and sent me gifts, but I didn't like him anymore and he couldn't understand why. One day, he showed up without any notice, thinking I would find this romantic. On campus, I saw a lot of romantic gestures arranged by guys for girls. As they understand it, women like to be chased and wooed. There was always a guy kneeling down and holding roses in front of a girl. Yang's chasing just annoyed me.

Shan, another guy from my high school, also asked me out. He wasn't quite my type: He was majoring in engineering and wasn't interested in the arts at all. I told him we could be friends, but then he called one night drunk, begging to be with me.

It happened a few times like that for me. When I said I just wanted to be friends, the guys would either chase me or get angry. I thought there had to be more to romance than a game of cat and mouse—I craved an authentic connection.

I did have a crush on someone: a boy from Lutai named Wei. Tall and with thick eyelashes, he was majoring in German at another university in Beijing. Because of him, I studied German during my free time, to have more to talk about when we met. We had known each other since we were thirteen years old. I spent a lot of weekends hanging out with him, and sometimes we'd take the long bus ride back to Lutai together.

QQ, an instant messaging app, had become popular, and I checked it every evening simply to see if Wei was on it. When I received a message from him, I'd get butterflies in my stomach. A lot of my journal was about him: what he said, what he did, and how I felt about him. I printed a photo he took for me, framed it, and put it on my desk. In a sense, he was my first love—though we were not together. We talked about everything. There was nothing that made me happier than being with him.

The more time we spent together, though, the more I wished he could take it one step further and ask me out, but it never happened.

Na's boyfriend came by almost every Friday afternoon and sat in the lounge waiting for her. He'd wave hi to me when I passed by. At night after classes and before going to bed, Na always stood in the corridor in her pink pajamas talking to him for hours. I longed to have that with Wei.

I never asked Wei about us. I was afraid our relationship would be ruined if he found out I expected more, if he

didn't. I preferred to keep it as it was rather than risk having
no relationship at all.

*   *   *

Still with no real love life, I could focus on my studies. My
parents had been supportive when I was choosing my major; they said I could study whatever I was interested in.
Most of my friends were not so lucky. I listed three choices:
Chinese literature, French, and Japanese, but my *gaokao*
score was not high enough for me to get into any of them.
So I was assigned to a finance major. I hated it, but I could
not refuse it. If I had, it would have meant another year in
high school so that I could retake the *gaokao*!

Our teachers said we "must learn to walk with two legs,"
for example, to major in finance and be skilled in English.
The goal was to make us competitive internationally. If I
had wanted to be a CFO of a Chinese company, my teachers would push me to learn English so that I could become
a CFO of an international Fortune 500 company.

Although the Chinese ideology of working "to serve our
country" was ingrained in us, in reality, that goal meant
little. What we wanted more than anything else was individual success, never mind the motherland. I thought working
in a top Western company would be good for me.

As a student in Beijing, I had more foreign exposure
than others studying elsewhere in the country, not just because of the cosmopolitan atmosphere of the capital and
its many tourists, but also because our university had so
many American and British lecturers. One of these was

Helen Smith, who insisted that we call her Helen, not Teacher Helen. An American from Mississippi, she was the first person I met who had blue eyes and light blonde hair. She was a devout Christian, so we learned a lot about Christianity from her. On Easter, Helen brought in paints and brushes and boiled white eggs for us to decorate. On Christmas Day, she held a party at her apartment. She taught us to sing "Silent Night" and "Santa Claus Is Coming to Town" and dressed up as a female version of Santa Claus. Helen had us over for movie nights, and it was there that I first watched *Star Wars* and *Back to the Future*. She encouraged me to read foreign newspapers even though I didn't really understand them, and would leave copies of the *New York Times*, the *Financial Times*, or the *Wall Street Journal* in our reading room. She gave me an English name, Karoline, that I would end up using in my writing career.

"I see great potential in you, Karoline. Don't be shy when you talk to me in English. You should be proud of yourself. Your English is much better than many Chinese people who have lived in America for years." I was fascinated by the foreign teachers like Helen and liked that she had given me a pseudonym. I told her I wanted to be a writer, and felt she believed in me. I thought, if there were angels, she was one of them.

Because of her encouragement, I became obsessed with learning English.

Barack Obama was then running for his first term as president of the US, and we would play recordings of his speeches to improve our listening comprehension. I thought he was handsome and intelligent, and I was intrigued by his African American heritage. He was doing so well, and his success gave me confidence: I should never think anything was impossible. If a black man could be president of the United States, I, a girl from a small town, could one day do great things in China.

Slowly, our idols ceased to be South Korean pop stars, and became European and American influencers. Yun greatly admired Steve Jobs and was the first girl in my class to buy an iPhone. Even Tian started to watch *The Big Bang Theory* and *Modern Family* instead of Japanese anime.

However, speaking English gave me headaches. I had never talked to any Western foreigners before coming to Beijing, and it was frustrating to communicate so hesitantly in another language, stumbling over grammar and vocabulary and pronunciation. I had a long way to go from knowing how to read the sentences to talking like a native speaker.

The day Barack Obama was elected, Teacher Jack Lee was so excited he gave a long speech. But I could only understand a few words: *Obama, president, proud, remarkable, black man, excited.* I had to guess at what he was saying, but by the time I figured it out, I had already missed the chance to celebrate with him.

Most of my classmates had grown up in Beijing, where English was often heard, or seen in advertising and in shops, so they had a head start because they talked to foreigners in the street and in their schools. No matter how many hours I immersed myself in English-language newspapers and magazines, it didn't help; I was a mess.

I thought making friends with English speakers would be the best way to improve, but the foreign students were mysterious. They lived together in the only dormitory building with an elevator. I heard two students, rather than six, shared one room! And they didn't have a curfew. I often heard music and shouting late into the night. They had a lot of parties. In the morning, we'd often see used beer cans crushed all over the ground outside their dorms.

Chinese students also drank, but instead of going to bars or in someone's room, we went to the private rooms of restaurants, and only with people we knew well. Going to bars and hanging out with strangers, even with acquaintances, was awkward and would warrant gossip.

One day Tian and I sneaked into a bar nearby. I had begged her to go with me because I was too nervous to go alone. Tian had nothing to do that evening and agreed. Although we were both over eighteen, the drinking age in China, she and I had never been to a bar. Only in a few big cities like Beijing and Shanghai were people starting to hang out in such places. Even today in Lutai there aren't any. Instead people go to teahouses. I confused bars with nightclubs, and didn't understand the difference. I also believed bars were noisy and dangerous for young women. The TV shows didn't help my thinking. In American TV shows, there was always a bad guy harassing a woman in a bar.

When Tian and I got inside, we found it full of foreigners. We looked completely out of place. People had dressed up for a birthday party. Three or four people stood or sat together in a group, drinking and laughing loudly. They wore dresses and makeup, and the guys were in leather shoes. It was a nightclub.

Tian and I sat down anyway and a man began staring at us, perhaps because we were dressed in sneakers and loose T-shirts and looked really lost. We didn't know how to order, because neither of us had ever touched any of these drinks. Reading the English menu made me dizzy.

"How can I help you?" the bartender asked. I pretended to be examining the drink names carefully. Beers? Cocktails? Or wine? I had no idea and turned to Tian. She looked around as if she didn't see me gawking at her. She wasn't helping. She stood behind me, like I was her protector. "I'll order the same thing as you," she finally said.

"A cocktail, maybe two, for both of us," I said. God knew how a cocktail tasted, but at least it looked pretty, and I had heard they were sweet.

"Which one in particular?" The bartender turned the menu to the pages where at least twenty different kinds of cocktails were listed. *Kill me,* I thought. *What are the differences?* The bartender must've noticed my confusion. I didn't want to look up at his grave face. A few foreigners were crowded around me, waiting for me to finish so they could get another drink. "Long Island and Bloody Mary, that's it," I said. The bartender gave me a face that said, *Are you kidding me?* But I didn't know what the problem was.

"Are you sure? It's a bit strong," he said.

"I'm sure," I said. My face was burning. I wasn't sure, but I didn't want to embarrass us. I glared back at Tian, but she seemed pretty relaxed and was scrolling on her phone, pretending to pay no attention to what was happening. I wanted to shout at her to get off the phone, but she wouldn't understand.

Tian and I took our drinks and retreated to a spot near the window. I was so self-conscious that I had forgotten how to walk. I started wobbling like a duck for some reason. The foreigners began to dance, stretching their arms and legs, like they were drunk. I didn't want to get any closer to them. Were they laughing at us? I wished there was a hole under the table that I could crawl into. It was a failure. I quickly finished my Long Island and pushed Tian to finish her Bloody Mary. She was coughing by the first sip. "Never mind, let's go!" I grabbed Tian, and we sneaked out quickly.

I was thankful to be out of there. I had a headache for the rest of the night.

My second attempt at experiencing an English environment was going to "English corners," where people discuss their opinions in English over a topic or two they select.

My friend Sun Bin introduced me to the English corners. Sun Bin came from a town, Chongyi, and was two years younger than most students in our class. He joked that he still had time to grow. He was small but disciplined like a soldier. He got up at six o'clock every morning and recited English essays from his textbook. He was one of the first to arrive in the classroom every day and always sat in the front row. He was keen to answer questions, and soon became one of the foreign teachers' favorites. One of them told him about an English corner at Wǔdàokǒu, and Sun Bin took me along.

Wǔdàokǒu was on the other side of the city. We went

through twenty stations on three different subway lines, the journey lasting two hours. People called Wǔdàokǒu "the Center of the Universe" because it was one of the most international places in Beijing. There were foreigners everywhere and from all over the world. It was common to see shops and cafés with signs in many different languages— English, Korean, French.

Wǔdàokǒu was also the cradle of tech start-ups and was rich with China's top IT tycoons.

The English corner Sun Bin and I attended was at a language training center. The owner held networking events that welcomed both foreigners and locals. Native English speakers were rare, so often a group of young Chinese people would surround a white person, saying how much they loved Hollywood movies and the Harry Potter series. They all had English names like Lucy, Nancy, Jack, or Tom, and some strange names like Cheery, Apple, Candy, and Strongman, either selected from television shows or made up because they liked the pronunciation.

The Chinese students' introduction was always in the same broken Chinese: "Hi, I'm here to make friends with foreigners. I like both Chinese and English culture." Then the same robotic questions came pouring out from the rest of us: "Why did you come to China?" "How long have you been in Beijing?" "Do you plan to stay long?" Their eyes would light up when the foreigner said something in Chinese like *xièxiè* or *búkèqi*, which meant "thank you" and "you are welcome."

"Your Chinese is great," the students would always say.

English corner helped, but it took too long to get there.

Instead, Sun Bin and I formed a group during lunchtime that included English-speaking staff.

The teacher I chatted with most during these discussions was Mike. He and his wife had retired from their jobs in the US and were traveling the world. He was a young-looking sixtysomething, his hair and beard half-gray; he played tennis and was a runner. He was a fan of history like me. One day over lunch, he said: "I doubt anyone in your class knows about June Fourth."

"I know!" I shouted with passion.

Mike and the other foreign teachers seemed both open-minded and critical of China, and enabled us to have the type of conversations we could not have elsewhere.

But to my surprise, Mike clammed up, simply returning to his noodle soup and avoiding looking my way. I kept probing him; he just kept sipping his soup.

Later I learned that every single foreign teacher had been warned against talking about it.

Since *junxun*, I had spent more time researching the events of June Fourth. On the Chinese websites, almost everything about the event was deleted or blocked. On Baidu—China's version of Google—when you typed in "June Fourth," the only results were the Chinese government reports that I had read a million times. The government blocked almost all major foreign news sites, so I had no way of finding more information.

Finally, Mike suggested that I use a VPN—a virtual private network—to log on to the blocked sites. Few people in my circle knew about or wanted anything to do with VPNs, and I remembered that I still had a VPN given to me by

Falun Gong members in high school during their anti-party movement.

That afternoon, I raced back to my room and had a friend help me install it. Instantly, I did a Google search and discovered photos and videos of students protesting in front of Tiananmen Square, holding banners that read "Liberty or Death" and "Democracy Saves China." A sculpture of the goddess of democracy had been erected, and students on the hunger strike sat under it. Military tanks and bloody people lay on the roadsides, fire and guns in the air. I learned that many protestors were still in jail or in exile, or had died. I cried as I watched my country's soldiers kill their own people, on the orders of our government. I thought about the photo I took in front of Tiananmen Square during my family's trip to Beijing. I was smiling. I was excited because there were a few soldiers standing behind me. I was so proud of the national emblems everywhere and of the characters posted above the gate: "Long Live the People's Republic of China." I had showed the photograph to all my friends. But now, thinking about the photo, I felt betrayed, my respect for the army seriously dented. China collapsed for me suddenly. I no longer understood what was in front of me. I had no faith in what I had been brought up to believe.

CHAPTER TWELVE

A Train of Dreams

When I returned home for Spring Festival, I was sullen and depressed, and impatient with my family. They seemed like such conformists, and I hated their naive questions about school and Beijing. They just wanted me to whet their palates with false hope so that they could continue to believe how beautiful and serene the capital was. They seemed like children to me. I told them it was not a magical place, it was just a place! I had experienced more darkness in the past six months in Beijing than in my previous nineteen years. I questioned everything my family did and said when I returned home, as if there were a gigantic question mark looming over my head. I had questions about government, systems, law and order; I was no longer a kid. I did not have blinders on, and I wanted theirs off too. I knew exactly who we were as villagers and as Chinese people under an oppressive government.

"She just has the freshman blues," my mom consoled Baba, who shook his head.

Then, two weeks before the new semester, Laoye passed away suddenly after a heart attack. My last grandparent was gone. The day we buried his ashes, we also burned the Falun Gong books he had kept hidden and his party membership card and placed these in the same urn.

After returning from the family gravesite, I locked myself in my room. When I was younger, like everyone else, I had been critical of him for his change of heart about the party. Now I understood that he had released himself from disillusion as I also had. He had been secretly practicing Falun Gong until the last stage of his life. I cried for him; he would have understood what I was going through. The rest of my family chose not to, but that was the Chinese way. Caiyuan's sky, a thick shield of gray, made me long for my grandfather's light.

When the festival was over, I again boarded the bus to Beijing, but this time on my own. I didn't need Yunxiang to take me. I was no longer the same scared girl I had been only a few months before.

Days passed in a blur during my second semester. I ran from one building to the next for classes, student union meetings, meals, lectures, and tests, and then I'd do it all again the next day. The repetition seemed monotonous, without excitement or rest. On the weekends, there was more work. My life's path had been overrated—as a student in the city, I had no more joy or fortune than a farmer in the village. My path grew more confusing to me with every test and every paper to manage. The days turned in and out of each other, over and over, like a dance I struggled to keep up with.

As June approached, one day my former *fǔdǎoyuán*,

Guan Xin, emailed the board of student leaders I was on, calling for an urgent meeting. Apparently, all universities in Beijing had come under intense pressure to make sure that nothing happened to mark the twentieth anniversary of June Fourth.

"You should set a good example for others and show the right political attitude. I trust you will stand with the government and not make a mistake," Guan Xin said.

I looked down and held my tongue.

He said there was a rumor that some students were planning to wear white T-shirts as a silent rebellion, and he didn't want to see any white clothes that day on campus. "Lastly, do not accept interviews from the awful foreign journalists."

We dutifully wrote everything he said in our notebooks.

On June 4, I switched on my VPN and sat in front of my laptop reading coverage of the anniversary on foreign newspapers and websites.

On campus, everything was quiet. We had classes as usual, and no teachers mentioned the special meaning of the date. At lunch, in the canteen, people watched *News 30 Minutes*, which covered everything from China's GDP growth to updates on the space program, but not a single word was mentioned about June Fourth. All seemed ordinary. In fact, it was all too ordinary. I wanted my friends and classmates to care about the anniversary as much as I did. I had sat in silence during Guan Xin's talk, and wrestled with myself all day. *I should have spoken up. I should have asked questions,* I thought. Instead, I had done exactly as I had been taught; I sat silently.

That evening, in my dormitory, I said to my roommates, "Don't you care that it's June Fourth? We should do something!"

"Why? What's the point?" Yun asked.

"All of us say we want democracy and freedom of speech."

"Yes, but I don't want to put myself at risk for a cause that most likely won't come true," Yun said in her elegant way.

"I don't like that you put yourself on the moral high ground," Mei said to me, "and assume that we don't care about it."

Yun and Mei were both from central Beijing. On the night of June Fourth, a bullet shattered the window of Mei's grandparents' house in the *hutongs* south of Chang'an Boulevard, near Tiananmen Square. Her grandmother, who had earlier sent food to both the students and the young PLA, was terrified. "She didn't even dare whisper," Mei said. "The soldiers and the students were the same age. Some students were killed, and so were the soldiers." Yun told me that her father had been an idealistic young man who listened to rock music and grew his hair long. In 1989, he was working in a state-owned soda factory but also protested against things that mattered to him. "He changed his tune after the government cracked down on the movement. The gunshots still haunt him," Yun said. "He warned me before coming here to never get involved in any political movements. He told me that nobody could help me if I got in trouble, not even him."

I had met her father on the first day of school. He ran

his own advertising company now, but I could see something heavy in his eyes, which looked tired and worn. Yun told me he drank a lot, to forget. His only goal now was to make money and send his daughter abroad and out of China.

"Protests will only bring more instability to your life," Yun said. "Leave the problems alone, Chaoqun. They'll solve themselves as China develops."

"I don't want to be in trouble for crimes against the government," Mei added. "That would be terrible for my family."

When the electricity in the dorm was cut off as usual at 11 p.m. it ended our discussion, for the most part. And though I was disappointed with my friends and other students for their passivity, I also hadn't done anything. It was painful for me to admit, but I guessed it did not make sense for me to risk my future either. We were taught to play the game and abide by the rules even when we didn't like them. From our first day in primary school, Chinese children are taught to be opportunists. If I were kicked out of the university for organizing a protest, my future would be ruined. We were not foreigners with endless opportunities. I only had one and needed to make the most of it. Before I closed my eyes to sleep, I climbed down from my top bunk, walked to the window, and lifted a corner of the curtain. A half-moon hung over the treetops. I imagined for a second what it might have been like on this night twenty years ago. When I crawled back into bed and lay down in peace, I was glad no one had protested and there wouldn't be any trouble.

★   ★   ★

"Do you want to settle down in Beijing in the future?" I asked Sun Bin while we were on the train traveling to our internships. I was going to the finance department of an international agricultural company; Sun Bin to an auditing firm.

"Everybody wants to," he said. "But it's difficult."

It was rush hour on a Monday morning. It was so crowded we had to stand and squeeze ourselves against the door.

"I know I won't go back to my hometown," he added confidently. "If not Beijing, then maybe Shanghai, Guangzhou, or Shenzhen. My goal is to be one of the city elites who can travel abroad a few times a year, afford a good education for my children, and never be afraid of becoming ill because I'll have health insurance. I'll have a big apartment."

I looked around at the other passengers. Many of them were male white-collar workers wearing plain black suits. They would commute for one or two hours to the city from their homes in the suburbs. Some might spend as many as six hours a day commuting round trip. And no matter how hard they worked, or how long their hours, many of them still wouldn't have the life Sun Bin described.

When we arrived at the next station, passengers waiting on the platform rushed to the door before it opened, pushing their way in. I was hardwired to the door. The subway staff in their blue uniforms yelled at the crowd to stand in line, but people struggled to get in and out anyway. A woman kept screaming into my ears, "Not out yet!" and held her purse tightly while squeezing out.

The announcements were in English and Chinese: "Welcome to subway line one." A little boy sitting on his mother's lap made me chuckle as he repeated the English words. Sun Bin moved his foot aside slightly as a man stamped on it when he turned around to get more space. The man didn't apologize. A fat woman was fighting loudly on her phone with someone. This was the morning hustle in Beijing.

I had never been passionate about my major, and any hope that I might like to work in finance was killed in that six-month internship.

Everything about the company looked professional and would have been nice for someone else, but not for me. The skyscraper was modern, and two very pretty, smiling receptionists welcomed guests and staff. Sunlight flooded into the tidy, clean offices. Chinese employees wrote and spoke to each other in English, though I didn't understand why at first. I sat in a room shared with junior employees. At lunchtime, the employees in their white shirts and tailored skirts chatted about their recent travels or the newest Louis Vuitton handbags. I wanted to join them but had nothing to contribute. I knew they were not interested in hearing my opinions on healthcare reform or equal rights for women. I could only imagine how they would look at me if I brought up such issues.

So I spent most of my time alone at my desk inputting data. As I punched in numbers, I realized I had to make a change. This kind of job might bring me money, but I

wouldn't get any sense of fulfillment, which to me was water to a fish. I finished the internship, knowing I would
never again work for a finance company. I would do what
my heart most desired; I would be a writer, a journalist.

★   ★   ★

I was down. I would soon realize that my choices would affect me in ways I hadn't foreseen. I still didn't know what
to call my relationship with Wei...that is, until he told me
he had a girlfriend.

I never asked him why we had never properly dated, but
I guessed one reason was that his parents didn't approve
of me. In Lutai, everyone knows everyone else. My parents
liked Wei, and they were even more eager than I was to
see us together, but Wei's mother had openly said things
against me, one of them being that I was too opinionated
to be a good daughter-in-law. My family said I should not
take her comments too seriously but I did, very seriously.
Her words hurt me. I liked having opinions and I liked
Wei. I hated that she wanted me to pick between him and
being myself. I was not a bad person, and I had no idea
why she disapproved of me so much. I had barely ever spoken to her.

One day Wei sent me a message on QQ:

Are you there? I have something important to tell you.

My heart started beating faster. I wondered if this was finally the moment he would ask me to be his girlfriend.

Listen, I have a girlfriend now.

You're my best friend, so you are the first one I wanted
to share this with.

A smiley face followed.

I felt a stabbing feeling in my heart, so much so that I
was certain that it was bleeding. I didn't answer him for a
few minutes, and then I lost control of myself and started
pouring out everything I had felt for him in the years we'd
been seeing each other. Tears dropped on my keyboard with
every word I wrote. And then I felt so angry with him, his
mother, and whoever this new girlfriend was.

He sent me a lot of messages back, but I didn't read any
of them.

My body ached, reflecting the ache in my heart, and I
was tired. I tried to close my eyes to sleep, but I couldn't. After a few hours' tossing and turning, I saw my phone light
up with a message from Wei.

Sorry if I hurt and misled you. I think we are very similar, and a couple should be different to make up for
each other's shortcomings.

What was that supposed to mean? I wanted to scream
at him. This was the reason? Had I shared too much with
him? Had too many opinions like him? Was I not meek
enough like his new girlfriend must be? Of course we were
alike; that's why I liked him! Couples were supposed to
have things in common. I tossed all night, recounting and

regretting everything I could possibly have done to make him think that way.

When I opened my curtain the next morning, the sky was covered in a blanket of thick gray smog. It had snowed two days ago, briefly clearing the air of pollution. Beijing's air pollution had grown worse over the years and now, after the snow, the toxic smog returned, burning my eyes and nose. My roommates complained, but today the smog was the perfect backdrop for my mood.

Tian stretched a pink paper mask over her mouth and nose before heading out to class. I had been suffering from allergies since I moved to Beijing. The coal-burning factories, a surge in the number of vehicles, and Beijing's topography exacerbated the situation. Surrounded by mountains, the city traps pollution. Smog is now related to nearly one-third of deaths in China, and reduces the life expectancy in northern China by three years. In the south, the air is much better.

We kept the windows closed and I planned to stay inside all day and think about what had happened, but Yun and Mei said it wouldn't do me any good to think about him a second longer. Christmas was approaching and they wanted to walk around the city. Although Christmas was not an official holiday, young people celebrated it. The funny thing is, we did not know or care about its origin. In China it had become an excuse to go shopping, and many malls and department stores were decorated for the Western festival.

There was a huge, waving blow-up Santa placed at the

front of the shopping mall, Joy City. Children wore reindeer ears, and couples took photos by Christmas trees decorated with tinsel. I wondered if Wei and his mysterious new girl-friend were doing the same. Strings of bulbs were twined on the trees, and an ad with a smiling Chinese housewife in a Christmas sweater was flashing on an electronic sign. I usually loved this time of year, but thoughts of Wei and his girlfriend made me so depressed, more and more alone, and like I would never fit in anywhere.

Christmas in China also had nothing to do with family, unlike in the US. It was a day for young people—friends and lovers. When I was in middle school, on Christmas Eve we'd collect twenty-four coins from our friends and buy a special apple wrapped in glittery paper and tied with a lace bow. The apple was bigger and redder than other apples we ate on regular days, and ten times more expensive. We'd give them to a boy or girl we liked or to a good friend.

I had no plans or interest in celebrating Christmas this year. Besides the falling-out with Wei, I had other things that bothered me. I found myself constantly stressed about having to make decisions. I was no longer a baby bird in the nest. Growing up in a traditional Chinese home, I was only taught how to study and behave. Those two principles took me only so far. Now, all the problems and pressures of real life, things I should have learned to handle by now, felt like an explosion. Suddenly my family wanted me to have a boyfriend, but I didn't know how to have a relationship—I had no experience. I had messed up with Wei and talked too much. I had made a foolish decision about my career plans. Journalism sounded exciting, but could I make enough money to feed myself? How could I train? And suppose I wanted children and a family? How attractive would I be if I were broke? I was at a crossroads.

I was due to be one of 6.8 million graduates, a new record. Few others would want to leave the city. Many, like me, had achieved a dream for their families by being here. To compete, I could try for master's programs, but I would have to pass another exam to apply, and it would take six months and more money to prepare. I could go abroad, but my parents couldn't afford to help me do that. There was a lot of competition for civil service jobs, such as in post offices, customs, tax bureaus, and courts, jobs with benefits, the possibility of promotion, and power. Civil servants could become government officials of cities and provinces. Sometimes, thousands of people would compete for one position. There was a civil service examination, but it was tough and didn't guarantee job placement. And besides, all I wanted to do was write.

When I finally mustered the courage to call my parents and tell them I had decided to try for a master's in journalism at Tsinghua University, they went from calm to explosive in a matter of seconds. "Why would you do such a ridiculous thing? After all this studying you've done? Stick with finance. If you're a government accountant, everybody will want to be like you."

"Not everybody, not me! It's boring, and I don't want my life to be like dull, stagnant water." I was a bit erratic and emotional, but wanted their approval.

"What's wrong with stability?" my mom asked. "Your father and I would be so happy to have stable jobs. Is a scattered life what you want? Then what's the university degree for?"

They didn't want me to have the same pressures they had.

They wanted me to find a job that could provide me with a Beijing *hukou*. I'd be able to buy a house and a car and have decent medical care, and my children could attend good schools in the city. I knew a girl who had turned down a well-paid job at a multinational corporation for a less glamorous job in Beijing, only because the latter promised a *hukou*.

I told them I would never sacrifice my happiness for a *hukou*. I wanted to live in Beijing but only if I could do a job I loved. At this point, I wasn't sure if I'd ever get married and have children. "Why should I worry about children who don't exist?"

"You're selfish," my mom said, about to hang up the phone. She had had enough.

Before she could hang up, I asked, "Would you be happy if Laolao had stopped you from leaving Caiyuan? Our situations might be different on the surface, but the issues are the same. I want to have a life that I believe is right and worth chasing."

She didn't respond. I knew we would both have a sleepless night after this—we rarely argued—and I felt more than ever that I was doing the right thing.

★   ★   ★

Our argument lasted for days. My parents made me promise to work in a state-operated news organization like *People's Daily*, a paper I criticized as the party's mouthpiece, but which to my parents and their friends was the best newspaper in China. This temporarily stopped the quarreling. However, six months of study later, I failed the exam to get into the journalism school.

I couldn't stand it. My parents' eyes were ready to pop when I went home and announced that I had no job or school or boyfriend. I could only imagine what they were thinking.

Maybe I should face the truth that I'm not a good writer, I thought.

The first six months of the final year in university are the best time to find a stable job. I had missed that opportunity, and was totally depressed about the mess I was in. I did not know what I had gained from being in Beijing. A good job would have been my one and only ticket to belonging there, but I had screwed it up. I had once thought that by working hard, everything would come to me. I was wrong. And now I was miserable, with no future plans— probably the worst thing ever for a Chinese woman my age. My mom had worked so hard for me, and I did not want to disappoint her. I thought about Laolao, who had never had opportunities to make any decisions about her own life. And look what I had done. I'd failed her, and my mom.

After everything I had done—working overtime in the library, skipping movies to study—I still wasn't good enough. Part of me felt as if I was still just a village girl and that Beijing and I were not compatible. My roommates seemed to have their lives sorted: Yun planned to go abroad. Tian, who had also failed a master's examination, would live at home and retake it next year. Na would marry her high school sweetheart and work at a local accounting firm. Mei got an offer from one of China's biggest banks, where her grandfather had once been director.

I started looking for a job in the last four months before graduation, like a madwoman scrolling through every recruiting website several times a day in a frantic search for an inkling of hope. Most big media firms had already finished the recruiting process. Looking at my résumé, I knew I was at a disadvantage: female, no Beijing *hukou*, and no journalism experience or degree. Most of the companies asked applicants to attach their photos on the forms. I guessed mine didn't help. Employers filtered their CVs: male, check; Beijing *hukou*, check; good-looking, check; rich parents, even better. I had none of those assets.

I realized how unrealistic my plan had been. I had never interned for media organizations, and I knew nobody. It was too late; I couldn't turn back.

As much as I wanted to be a journalist, I also questioned how fulfilling it would be to work as one in China with so much censorship: Topics like Tibet, ethnic minorities, and any criticism of the government and the party were sensitive; and though not officially forbidden, they were usually problematic, but I had felt a shift. Not all the media was directly state-owned. After Reform and Opening Up, the market expanded to independent publishers. Bold journalists, at relatively liberal outlets, wrote about topics related to human rights, activism, and political reform, though they still had to do it subtly and cautiously. Investigative reporting was becoming increasingly popular.

The internet had provided journalists with a platform to expose more of the truth that had been hidden previously. In response, China's propaganda department hired two million people to police the internet and report cybercrimes and anti-Communist speech and opinions. But information could spread like wildfire and was less easily controlled. It was the peak of the Chinese media's shift, and I so desperately wanted to be part of it. Time was on our side, and news could go viral before it was caught and censored.

Eventually I had a phone interview with Xingguang Media, who were looking for someone to write press releases for their clients. I was so desperate and it was much closer to journalism than an accounting job, so I took it. At least it was media-related. Everything was going fine until the human-resources manager, a man with a shrill, rasping voice, asked, "When are you going to get married? I need to plan ahead for your maternity leave."

Instantly, my blood started to boil.

"I don't know," I said slowly between clenched teeth. "I don't even have a boyfriend."

"I'm afraid you're going to work here for a year and then take time off for a baby. I'll need you to sign an agreement stating that you're not going to do that."

"How can I sign that? I can't predict the future."

He added: "We wouldn't want to waste each other's time."

In China, speed reigned: Couriers took shortcuts to save thirty seconds; teachers highlighted the "important sections" in books and discouraged students from reading anything that wouldn't be on the test. Chinese people probably invented speed dating; they wouldn't hesitate to ask each other's age, job, *hukou*, and savings-account balance the first minute they met.

I didn't want my work and biological clock to be mapped out for me, so I politely refused to sign the document, but this meant I could no longer work there. I never spoke to the HR man again.

So there I was again, without a job as graduation day approached. The lack of a job felt as if there were a time bomb sitting on my shoulder. I was sweaty and nervous, a complete wreck. I could barely function. At night, I'd wake up feeling as if a pair of scissors were cutting me into pieces. To my family and friends, I had always been a model student and source of pride. Now I'd end up graduating without a job to go to? I hated to disappoint my parents, especially after I had fought for them to believe in me. I felt stupid and terrible. I'd have to leave Beijing ASAP. It was expensive, and I couldn't ask my parents for more money.

When my mother called, I tried to convince her in a lighthearted tone that I was fine. Sun Bin suggested I try again to find an accounting position, which had lots of jobs advertised. So I told my mom I would do that, even if in my heart, I didn't want to. When Mom and I finished talking, I walked to the highest floor of the dorm. From there, I could see the lights sparkling in distant towers, the stream of cars, and bright blinking dots of airplanes waiting to land in the international airport. *If Beijing is so big, why isn't there a place for me?* I often thought. Maybe I aimed too high and wanted too much. Maybe dreams were just a luxury, or a star I would never reach.

CHAPTER THIRTEEN

Foreign Territory

Five days before graduation, I saw an online advertisement posted by the English-language magazine *That's Beijing,* which was looking for a writer to cover social and cultural news, and be able to deliver copy in English. That was the job for me! I doubted they would take me on with no experience, but I had nothing to lose. I created a Gmail account because I heard that would be more impressive, sent an email with my résumé and writing samples to Mary, the editor in chief, and changed my email signature from Chaoqun to Karoline. I laughed at myself for trying so hard to cater to Western standards, but Mary replied to me the next day.

I took a bus to the office, which was located in a high-end residential compound called Sun City.

I knocked. A thirtysomething woman who looked to be from Central Asia opened the door without looking at me. She quickly returned to her desk and left me there. A dozen people in the office were sitting at their desks, either typing fast or talking on their phones. There were three foreign women in the room in addition to the Asian woman. I wondered which one was Mary, but I was afraid to interrupt. I just stood there like a lost puppy.

A Chinese-looking man saw me. "What are you looking for?" he asked in terrible Mandarin. He emphasized every syllable with too much effort, and it sounded unnatural.

"Mary...," I stammered in English. I thought it might make him more comfortable.

"I'm Kenny, the marketing director," he said in American-accented English, now with a big smile on his face.

A blonde woman in her mid-twenties stood up and waved at me: "Hi, you must be Karoline."

This was Mary.

The magazine was using a two-bedroom apartment as the office, the living room an open space for editorial and sales, with two rows of white Ikea desks lined up next to each other. On the desks were magazines, computers, and leafy-green plants. One bedroom was an office for the accountants and HR department. The other was used as a small meeting room. Mary told me they also had offices in Shanghai, Guangzhou, and Shenzhen and were hiring for the city section, which carried the most feature stories.

"The most interesting part," Mary said, smiling.

She sent me home with copies of the magazine so that I could study its style, and told me to email her three story ideas. That afternoon, I emailed Mary with not three, but six ideas. The next morning, I had the job. The minute I got the email, I went flying out of my dorm room in tears and immediately called my parents. "I've got a job!" I said between wet sobs. My dream had come true. I had been right; I could do what I was passionate about. My insistence on being myself had finally paid off.

★   ★   ★

Suddenly my life didn't look like the one I had grown used to. I was no longer a student but the independent woman I had always wanted to be. The magazine sent me to cover fancy events, including an Indian food festival at the Ritz-Carlton, and I spent a lot of time trying new restaurants and nightclubs—and now I knew which cocktails to order (or not!) from the menu. Many nights were full of parties and drinking. I took taxis everywhere and my expenses were reimbursed. All my friends envied my lifestyle—which was pretty incredible! I was becoming more sophisticated, partly out of necessity: I learned how to eat with a fork and knife, knew the difference between good and bad coffee, and was meeting people from all over the world. But I was still the nervous village girl inside. Nobody was around to tell me what to do—no teachers, no parents, no rules, and I hated myself for sometimes missing that security. At the same time, I was restless and eager to get rid of the bookish schoolgirl in me.

It took a long time; I didn't know how to behave. I was the only Chinese member of the editorial team and the youngest in the office. I wanted to write more but worried that my writing in English was not good enough and would add more to Mary's editing workload. The fact that English was not my first language was an issue.

I also noticed how I was discriminated against for being Chinese. At first, I thought I wasn't invited to certain events because of my Chinese accent, but then I noticed that it was because I didn't have a white face. It was especially important to the head of sales, a Chinese woman whose English name was Claire. I never knew her age, but I guessed maybe she was in her thirties. She had long curly hair and always wore bright red lipstick.

Claire held tons of client events that she needed writers or editors to accompany her to. About one-quarter of the magazine was advertorial, which paid for our wages and other overheads, so her job was important. As a new employee, I had much more free time than my colleagues, but Claire never asked me along. If other people in sales asked me to go, Claire looked annoyed. She said I was too young to impress their clients. What she really meant was that I was too Asian.

One day Claire asked my UK colleague, Rob, to go to a fashion party with her at the Westin Hotel. It was production week and Rob had tons to do, so he insisted I go instead.

"What? I can't just take a Chinese girl to this *very* important party!" Claire yelled after a few rounds of arguments with Rob.

But aren't you also Chinese? I wanted to say. I found it ridiculous that I was being discriminated for my Chineseness in my own country. Claire had probably forgotten that she was one of us. She liked *laowai*, a blanket term we used (sometimes as an insult) when referring to foreigners, and by working with them, Claire thought she was superior to other Chinese people. She spoke more English than Chinese, and even cursed in English, which astonished me.

Although I despised her way of thinking, I understood where it had come from. She was a product of China. The clients believed that if there were a few foreign faces at their events, it meant their events were international, and that was enough. Conversely, for the Chinese parties, the more *laowai*, the better. White people are often hired by Chinese for events just to stand there and be white. White people are paid to appear in forums, lectures, and ceremonies, posing as doctors, professors, and other professionals. No skill is needed. They are sometimes given speeches to recite. It all makes the company or organization look good. When Chinese parents look for tutors for their children, they prefer European or American *laowai*, even if those people are from France or Poland and aren't native English speakers. They'll choose them over Chinese tutors, even Asian Americans.

Claire didn't care if the person she brought with her could write well or not. She only needed a mascot.

On the day of the party, after work, I waited for her to get ready. She spent over an hour doing her makeup in the bathroom. It felt like forever. "Did you bring anything else to wear like I told you? You can't just look like a poor student at this party!"

"Got it! I'll change after you are done!" I had spent 400 yuan on a strapless black dress. It was one-tenth of my monthly salary. *I must be crazy,* I thought when I bought it.

When Claire came out, she was wearing a pair of stilettos and a cream-colored dress that reached down to her ankles. I quickly rushed into the bathroom to change.

"Let's go, girl!" Claire walked out without looking back at me. Her right hand was holding a little round mirror, and she used her left hand to wipe a bit of lipstick from her teeth. She managed to wave and stop a taxi at the same time.

The cabs barely moved at this time of the day. Drivers cursed and honked their horns. I almost wanted to chicken out when we arrived, but kept telling myself I had to be confident in front of Claire. I walked straight as I could, looking forward, resisting everything that tempted me to stop and look in the grand hotel: the gleaming crystal chandelier, the musicians playing Debussy's "Clair de Lune," the guests wearing expensive suits and speaking softly in languages I couldn't understand, the fresh roses and lilies so beautifully arranged in a huge vase, resting on a table in the lobby. I had never been to any place like it.

Claire called someone over, and a woman walked toward us, swaying her hips like a flower in the wind. When she came closer, I admired her long green-velvet dress and her shimmering green earrings and necklace. *Compared with them, I must look like a peasant,* I thought. Claire introduced me as "our little editor, Karoline." The woman gave me the neat, symbolic smile I saw on the face of every woman like her. "I'm Vivian," she said and then hugged me. That was the only exchange I had with her. She and Claire talked all the way to a room where the party was going on. I just followed.

Champagne bubbled in flutes, warm yellow light reflected on the marble floors, and waiters in swallow-tailed coats held trays with fine hors d'oeuvres that looked like works of art. It reminded me of the parties in *The Great Gatsby*, and I was a Chinese Nick Carraway.

I knew no one, so I just walked around, holding a glass of champagne, and tried to understand those making speeches onstage. My fancy drink was just for decoration to help me pretend I fit in and was having a good time.

Most people at the event were foreigners. I knew there was a hierarchy among Beijing's expat community. People asked "where do you live?" more often than "what do you do?" because their addresses would reveal their status without being too direct. If they lived in the Diplomatic Residence Compound, they immediately were popular and everyone wanted to talk to them. Living in such a compound meant there was a big chance they were diplomats or foreign correspondents, one of the most popular expat professions in Beijing. I'd already been to plenty of parties where foreign hipsters would tell me they humbly lived inside Second Ring Road, in many old *hutong*s that were slowly being restored and had become very fashionable, and how they wanted to become the next Peter Hessler, the American writer famous for his books about China. But they couldn't wait to tell me they paid more rent than the migrant workers who also lived there, and that their houses had an indoor bathroom, not like the rest of their neighbors who had to share the public toilet. I began to understand that they wanted a taste of Old Beijing culture, but not its inconveniences. The Central Business District had the most foreign businessmen, and Shunyi was the home for English teachers working at the international schools. English teachers were only a little superior to the foreigners half their age living in Wǔdàokǒu, the international students' paradise.

I approached a group of three people talking near a window. A young French woman with brown hair and full lips was complaining about how difficult it was to date in Beijing. "You know here it is heaven for foreign men. I can't compete with local women, can I?" Noticing me standing near her, she looked a bit abashed. I pretended I had heard nothing, and talked to a Chinese American man who had just moved to Beijing as an event organizer for one of the biggest nightclubs. But I soon regretted it. He went on and on about how worried he was every day about something killing him: The water and food were poisonous, cars didn't obey traffic rules, and the electric wiring in his apartment was too old, but the landlord refused to check it properly.

"Yes, I understand." I tried hard to be patient. "So, then, what tempted you to come to China in the first place?"

"It's easy to find a job here as a foreigner," he said without blinking. Before I could respond, he continued, "You know what's most annoying? That Chinese people always speak Chinese to me." He chuckled. "I often have to say, 'Excuse me, I'm not Chinese.' Well, I am Chinese, but American Chinese…"

Whatever he was trying to say was not sinking into me or was completely full of contradictions, and I wanted him to get out of my face ASAP.

Claire had become rather tipsy, so I went with her outside to hail a taxi. I put her inside first and jumped in after.

So happy to leave, I thought.

"Ten years, ten years working as a saleswoman in Beijing. I've moved five times; finally I'm inside Second Ring Road," she mumbled. The Second Ring was the most expensive. She turned her face to me, and said with a mysterious smile, "As an older sister, I'm going to tell you something: It's fine to flirt with foreigners, but never get serious. It's the lesson I learned. None of the foreigners in Beijing are good people...none of them...Who would want to move from a comfortable developed country to a shit hole?"

It was impossible to have a real conversation with her at this point, so I only nodded.

When I got "home" to the room I was renting in Dingfuzhuang—not a fashionable area but affordable—it was almost one in the morning.

I recalled Claire's comments and thought them funny coming from her of all people. She had many foreign boyfriends, and I was sure she was dating one now. I was also dating a man from the UK. It was not a secret, but I didn't like to broadcast it to everybody in the office.

His name was Andrew, and we had met at a dinner with a mutual friend, James. That night I asked James to dinner because I was working on a piece about religion and he had done some research on the topic. When I arrived at the restaurant, James said he had asked another friend to join us.

Soon, a man with a ginger beard approached our table.

He was thin and his legs looked long in his dark blue jeans. I liked his brown-leather watchband. He had a square face, and through his glasses I noticed passion in his eyes. His beard looked redder in the candlelight.

He looks like a fox, I thought.

"Andrew, this is Karoline. You're both writers."

Andrew, who was from the UK, said he was in Beijing working on a book about Chinese youth. He said he had read my articles in *That's Beijing* and liked them. I was flattered, but not convinced. I had heard that the British could be deceptive, though aiming sometimes to be polite—it was their way of saving face—so when they said *interesting*, they might actually mean "boring."

My English skills were only good enough to deal with one native speaker at a time. When the two of them talked, I found it hard to follow, so I just sat quietly. Before we left, Andrew opened the door for me, and gestured for me to go first. I didn't know any Chinese men who did things like that.

A few days later, he sent a text asking if I wanted to go to a Halloween party with him.

Of all the Western holidays, Halloween confused me the most. I didn't understand why a group of adults would dress up in weird costumes or as ghosts and demons. I decided to wear a tight red dress, a pair of long red-silk gloves, and black high heels. I asked my hairdresser to tie up my hair, which I topped with a crown. I had no idea what my costume was. The hairdresser said I looked like Audrey Hepburn in *Breakfast at Tiffany's*. I laughed and decided to go with that.

When I arrived at the party, I knew my costume would be the last thing people talked about, which was a relief. Look-alikes of Harry Potter, Chairman Mao and a Red Guard, Catwoman, Lara Croft from *Tomb Raider*, and even the infamous BBC host Jimmy Savile, who had been accused of sexually assaulting minors, were there. The DJs pumped pop music, and I bopped along awkwardly while I waited for Andrew.

At about nine o'clock, I saw him come in. He wasn't dressed up at all! When he approached me, I looked into his blue eyes and saw their fire again. I knew that dating a foreigner would be the worst idea now if my goal was to settle down and work, but I couldn't help feeling excited about him. Chinese girls who dated foreigners were often perceived as bad girls or opportunists looking for visas or green cards. Since I wasn't seeking either, my family would think I was unhinged. But I had the right to be with whomever I wanted, and so we began seeing each other.

We watched old films together, went to clubs and jazz bars and to lectures given by famous authors visiting the city. Andrew's friends invited us to their barbecues. He carried a small notebook everywhere he went and kept a copy of the *New Yorker* on his desk. He had graduated from Oxford, and it seemed as if he had read every book and knew everything. I felt like I was falling in love with him.

After dating for weeks, I wanted to know if we were serious. To me, if he had not formally asked me if we were boyfriend and girlfriend, we were just friends. Because of my experience with Wei, I had to be more cautious.

The more I liked him, the more I worried. I asked a British friend about it. A Chinese guy would have already asked me to be exclusive long ago; each day that went by drove me crazy with anxiety.

My British friend said there wasn't such a rule in the UK.

"Then how do you know if you're boyfriend and girlfriend?"

"Somehow you know."

"Then what if the woman thinks they're in a serious relationship, and he thinks they are not. Could he date other people?" Of course I was thinking about Wei.

"In the beginning, it's not against the rules if you date different people," he said. "That's why people date, right? To meet different people, and see if one of them could become someone for a long-term, serious relationship."

I did not like this Western way of dating.

Another reason why I wanted to be sure is because I had the impression that Andrew wanted to go further than a kiss. I was curious, but wondered, if one day I got married to someone else, would my future husband mind that I had sex with other men? I knew that as a modern woman I should not care about such bullshit, but unfortunately, I still did. It would be me who suffered the consequences and judgment, not Andrew.

Soon after my confusing conversation with my friend, I found myself lying in bed with Andrew on Valentine's Day.

I could see the shadow of the trees out the window. It looked like a fairy tale and I felt as if I had finally met my prince. A few cats were howling on the roof, and his neighbor's dog was barking at them. Andrew caressed me like he always did, and I decided to tell him that I was ready. I felt in great control of my own body, and this was the feeling I wanted when losing my virginity. Whether Andrew was a foreigner or not, I knew that once again I would choose to go for what I wanted and not what Chinese tradition wanted for me. I would not regret it. I didn't want to be a perfect porcelain piece waiting for somebody to pick me up from a market shelf; I wanted to be a new woman, and experience life to the fullest.

CHAPTER FOURTEEN

"A Leftover Woman"

I bought Song, Chunting's son, a panda hat for his fourth birthday. He put on the hat, walked to the mirror, giggling, and came back to thank me with a kiss. My heart melted. Although I had been against Chunting's decision to have him, he had grown to be just as important to me as she was.

Chunting and Ling lived with his mother, Xianglan, in Houmi Village. Chunting was now a housewife. Ling delivered chicken guts from a slaughterhouse to the local fish farm and earned 500 yuan a day—a good wage, which he could supplement by working over the weekends, and more than most people his age earned, even those with a university degree. But his boss never paid Ling the full amount. Like many other laborers, Ling had no written contract, and his boss would invent all sorts of excuses not to pay him on time and in full. Chunting complained a lot if Ling didn't bring home the money that he was due.

"You will understand why money matters once you're married," Chunting scolded me when I asked her why she was giving Ling such a hard time.

In Houmi, everyone knew she had been pregnant when they got married. Though young people thought little of it, older people gossiped about them. But *guangguns*, unwed and childless, were even more embarrassing to their parents than an unplanned pregnancy. A grandson was a grandson, after all. As the old saying went, "Those who couldn't pick the grapes from the vine always said the grapes were sour."

Chunting and I met less often now that she had a four-year-old son and I was working in Beijing. But whenever I went home, we would spend a night or two together. We both found it difficult to fathom each other's lives, so we would talk long into the night. My decision to be a journalist was alien to her. Her decision to settle into factory work bothered me. I tried not to be disappointed in her, and was infuriated that she felt the same about me. She talked about money endlessly, and all her decisions seemed to revolve around it. Money didn't mean as much to me as a job that I could be proud of. But almost no one around me seemed to understand that—not my parents, my former classmates, and not my cousin and best friend, Chunting. The mutual disapproval grew and grew and almost became like a knife between us. Though we loved each other, we didn't agree on anything. I thought she was conforming, and she thought I was foolish. No matter where our conversation started, we always ended up back in the same place.

As we sat flipping through magazines one night, I told Chunting I was going to be in a play called *The Leftover Monologues*, inspired by the American writer Eve Ensler's *Vagina Monologues*.

She was baffled.

"Vagina, what?" she blurted out.

I tried to hide my irritation by explaining that it was a collection of stories about gender, sex, relationships, marriage, and being a woman in modern China.

"Leftover women" refers to those who haven't married by the time they reach twenty-eight years old. The term was all over the media, constantly in my face. I was immediately sickened by it. To call women "leftovers" was to stamp them with a fate of being lesser, an object that could be thrown away, as if women had an expiration date like food on a supermarket shelf, with no value greater than the age of their bodies.

No matter how hard I studied and worked, it didn't matter. At twenty-five, I was getting closer and closer to my "expiration date." The pressure was not only on me, and the stigma that my parents would face with a leftover daughter haunted me every day. I thought about it all the time, and was reminded of it everywhere. The play would help me become a part of a community of women who thought as I did.

Feminist notions of empowerment and equality were entirely new to me, as they were for many other young Chinese women, but they also felt like home. Feminism was also stigmatized, but I had watched my mom and Laolao and knew they had traveled quietly on the same path and suffered alone. I loved the community of feminists I met when doing the play.

Chunting listened to me go on and on about the play and the importance of China's feminist movement. Then she said, in annoyance: "All that stuff doesn't matter."

I wanted to scream and run out the door. We had been so close growing up, and now she had become just the kind of woman I didn't like.

Many of my friends and family in the village also didn't like my newfound ideas. They believed feminists were trying to upend traditional expectations between men and women and that the old customs were the best expression of love. Ads on TV and in shopping malls reminded Chinese women every day that, as they aged, their value declined. Whether it was the latest hair-color product or anti-aging creams, everything was sold as a way for women to stay beautiful in order to be loved, and to make sure their husbands never left.

While Chunting thought this meant women should be treated "as delicate as a flower," the old ways sounded more like punishment or imprisonment to me. But such values were widely subscribed to, so at times I questioned myself.

I had tried to keep my distance from feminism, but a nascent feminist movement was taking shape in China, mostly in the big cities. Leaders of the movement advocated against domestic violence, sexual harassment, and gender discrimination—all serious issues that were otherwise rarely talked about. After knowing what happened to Laolao's generation with the foot binding and lack of schooling, and all that Mom had been through with the One-Child Policy, I felt strongly about making changes for my own generation and for those in the future.

I was taught that a good girl should be considerate, loyal to her partner, and demure. I was told to pay close attention to my appearance. Boys, on the other hand, were encouraged to be strong, sporty, decisive, and independent. In high school, the girls were always scolded and told to "respect themselves," an indirect way of saying "remain abstinent," but the boys never suffered the same humiliation. Few women made it to top government positions or boardrooms; after all, they were "delicate flowers" and unsuited for those jobs. And even though statistically girls tended to outperform boys academically, it was implied that the boys had "greater potential." If they studied or worked harder, they would soon surpass the girls. A successful man was rewarded for his hard work; a successful woman was just lucky.

My parents treated Yunxiang and me mostly equally, but their expectations for us still differed. They believed Yunxiang's priority should be his career, while mine should be finding a successful husband and having loving children. As soon as I made it to university, my mom shifted her focus from my academic life to my love life. Each time when I went home, my conversation with her would go into relationship talk within ten minutes. No matter how I tried to change the subject, Mom turned it back. She worried that all the good men would be taken soon if I didn't rush myself into the competition. She also worried about my biological clock: "A woman's time is very valuable. Soon your eggs will not be as healthy."

Each time I had a new date, I had to keep it secret; otherwise, she'd insist on seeing his photo, and if I went on more than three dates, she would urge me to bring him home to meet her.

"That play sounds like a group of old ladies complaining about their husbands and sons," Chunting joked. "You'd better not become a leftover woman."

"How could you repeat that?" I shot back, now red with anger.

She looked at me for a long time. She had grown accustomed to this new side of me, the one who could get so fired up about social issues, but I could not help but protest her ignorance. I just couldn't sit there and accept it. I didn't care that she was my cousin, that we had played together in the snow and had bathed together when we were little. I wanted Chunting to change her ways, just as I wanted China to change, but she wouldn't. Then, suddenly, I saw a glimpse of hope.

"Yeah, it is a bit insulting," she said, as if realizing this for the first time. Then she smiled, suddenly playful again. "Is it serious with the guy you're dating? If not, better to end it and find someone else."

★   ★   ★

The truth was, Andrew and I had split up. I felt our relationship lacked something, or that maybe I wasn't confident enough to feel like his equal. Andrew's father was a renowned history professor, so Andrew had grown up in an intellectual household and he seemed to know about so many things I didn't. While discussing issues that appeared in Western newspapers with Andrew, I felt stupid all the time. I admired and loved Andrew a lot, especially when he talked about literature, politics, and art, but his eloquence and talents also made me feel bad about how little I could offer in exchange. I had no idea what he really thought of me, and I was jealous of all the female friends he had, though his research allowed him to meet a lot of people. He was busy working on his book and spent most of his time writing or traveling around the city doing interviews. Instead of openly talking about my doubts and concerns, I chose the typical Chinese route: to be silent and swallow my bitterness. My submissive behavior with him astounded me, but there was a simple reason for it: I felt small compared to him. He was three years older. He had seen more of the world than I had, read more books, had more friends. I never talked about my own family or friends. What could I say? My grandfather had plowed fields and raised cows—that couldn't be as interesting to him, or so I imagined. Rural life was often portrayed as idyllic in foreign films, but nobody wanted to know the truth of it: just poverty and more poverty—chained to the land, with a relentless cycle of chores day after day.

I was often critical of the government to my Chinese friends and family. With Andrew, I was the opposite. I found myself constantly defending my country. It was easy for me to put him and myself in two unfriendly positions. I couldn't help but side with the China he was criticizing. He probably thought I was a crazy nationalist. I usually regretted being so irritated with him, but I couldn't help it. I was afraid he would never truly understand me, given our different backgrounds. It was neither one of our faults.

Nine months after our first date, one Friday afternoon, Andrew asked me out for a walk after work.

It was windy outside, and it looked as if it were going to rain.

He was waiting for me in Raffles City, a nearby shopping mall. I hadn't seen him for more than a week. He didn't greet me with a hug as he usually did. We sat close together in a milk tea shop. He ordered me a fruit drink with ice cream.

"I'm going to Hong Kong this weekend to attend a friend's wedding," he began.

I nodded, and saw that his eyes looked a little red. I waited for him to continue.

"I have something to tell you," he said, and I waited. "You're a great person. We are similar in many ways, but we are also very different. I've given it a lot of thought and…there's no future for us. I know this will hurt, but the sooner we split up, the better it is for you."

A few years earlier, Wei had said we were too similar to be a couple, and now Andrew said we were too different.

Tears fell down my face, but I didn't say anything. I couldn't let him feel I wanted him too much. I grabbed my coat and fled. Andrew was chasing me but I didn't stop; I knew what I was doing. I wanted to get out, to get into a taxi. I ran and ran through the cars on Second Ring Road. He was behind me shouting something. I finally found a cab and went home.

It was true, he had hurt me, but I decided to swallow the bitterness.

CHAPTER FIFTEEN

Ten Hours for Eighty Yuan

I'd like to think it was all my feminist talk that inspired Chunting to get a job and depend less on her husband, but that was far from the truth. For Chunting, it was always about the money. The moment Song was old enough, she went back to work.

In the spring of 2016, when Song was six years old, Chunting found a job at the nearby Senyuan Leather Shoe Factory, which made products for export to the US and was only ten minutes from her home. The job did not provide paid holidays or health insurance or allow for time off: She had to work on the weekends. And of the three hundred working on the shop floor, only fifty were men. Many men preferred jobs at the steel or cement-making factories, or trucking, where physical strength could earn them a higher wage. "These men are all losers," Chunting confided in me, "either too weak or too lazy to find a better job."

In reality the shoe factory was a poor choice for everyone, women included. Chunting thought working in a factory selling American products meant added value, but it was the same as working in a factory anywhere else.

The shop floor had seven sections: leather cutting, gluing, stitching, hole punching, quality control, pair counting, and boxing. "Americans must be huge," Chunting told me. "No one in China wears shoes this big."

Chunting started by cutting leather, and then after a month she moved up to stitching. Her feet would push the sewing machine pedal under her desk, and she used her fingers to adjust the direction of the leather under the needle. About fifty machines operated at the same time; the noise swallowing Chunting's thoughts until her brain felt empty. "It feels like I am a machine," she joked. No one wore earplugs. As part of a production line, Chunting's hours were 8 a.m. until 6 p.m. Once again she felt trapped.

The longest-serving workers were disdainful of new recruits and gave Chunting a hard time. They were also jealous of anyone who achieved a higher rate of pay. One woman who had been at the factory for five years could now perform all the most difficult jobs most efficiently. In her hands, a flat sheet of leather quickly morphed into a shoe. So she was paid more. She wore headphones while she worked and never spoke to anybody. Others became so jealous they refused to do the preparatory work for her, leaving her without leather.

Chunting was positioned on the line between two of these resentful workers, whose job was to feed her similar-size shoe parts, placed together before they got to her so that she could sew them together. Instead of matching up the parts, the women would just heap them over in a jumble.

Chunting tried to talk to their supervisor, but she warned Chunting that her more experienced co-workers would likely take revenge for any repercussion and make it worse for her. "In my experience, after you've been here for a while, they'll be nicer to you," she advised. "Just wait until other newcomers join."

* * *

On a weekend when I visited Chunting, I spent half a day at another factory where she had been moved to. It was smaller, and felt more like a workshop, with only about twenty sewing machines and thirty workers. It was operating illegally, having been closed down for using coal-fired stoves in the winter to stay warm. When the local environmental protection bureau came for a surprise inspection, they discovered the stove and its chimney. They ordered that it be destroyed immediately and the factory shuttered. The owners paid the police tens of thousands of yuan to avoid jail time.

Though the government sealed the front door with a notice, "Failed the environmental protection test," the factory kept going—it was an open secret. Workers just entered through a side door.

Beijing's notorious air pollution was partly due to the country's industrial development and the factories set up in towns and villages surrounding the city, as well as sand storms that blew in regularly. To clean the air, the city government ordered almost every one of those factories closed, which would have meant a debilitating loss of jobs.

In reality, the local officials put on a show: Manufacturing contributed to economic growth. So, sometimes they destroyed stoves, and often they turned a blind eye to illegal operations.

Local officials decided to re-inspect the factory where Chunting was now working, but her boss had been forewarned. When the inspectors were due to arrive, she and the other thirty workers ran out to the cornfield to hide, locking the factory door behind them. The next week, as subterfuge, they worked from 5 to 11 p.m.

The factory smelled overwhelmingly of glue. Nobody wore a mask. Chunting was going to wear one, but feared it would make her look weak.

"Don't worry," she said to me. "After ten minutes you won't smell anything."

It was true. But my head began to ache, whether from the smell or from the noise of the sewing machines, I could not be sure. The machines were so loud that workers only spoke when they needed something, and when they did, they had to shout. I sat down quietly beside Chunting.

She worked seated upon a small, four-legged plastic stool, almost child-size, her face inches from the machine.

"You have to get your fingers close. I've been pricked by the needle twice this year," Chunting said, showing me her left index finger. "A needle broke the other day and flew off, hitting me in the face, but thankfully it hit my glasses." I noticed she was the only one in the workshop who was nearsighted. The glasses made her look more like a schoolteacher than a factory worker. "Being hit by a needle is nothing compared to being cut by a knife when you're cutting leather. One of those almost sliced straight through my finger."

I found it odd that she recounted these accidents in the same tone she used to count vegetables, and told her so. "Please," I added, "stay away from needles and knives." And with that, we looked at each other and cracked up.

That month they were making waterproof Wolverine shoes. A quick search on my phone revealed that the brand could sell one pair for 1,500 yuan, then worth about twenty days of Chunting's salary. This unnamed factory would produce the uppers of about three hundred pairs of shoes per day. After that they would be transported to another factory where the soles were added, then shipped to Europe and the US.

By 2010, China had replaced Japan as the world's second-largest economy, a development fueled by tens of millions of anonymous workers like Chunting, the underpaid and overworked shadows behind clattering machines. In that factory, I suddenly began to understand why my cousin cared so much about money. Who was I to judge her values from my air-conditioned office in the capital, with my lunch breaks and paid holidays?

After a while, I had to get some fresh air. The blue sky was scattered with clouds. Such beautiful days used to be rare during winter in northern China, so maybe the government's work was paying off, I thought. Yellow reeds swayed gently in the breeze, and a flock of sparrows had alighted on dry silver flowers.

After work, as Chunting and I walked home, her boss zoomed by in a BMW.

"Look at that," she said, "I work so hard, but I will never have that. It's not fair."

★   ★   ★

"I have something to tell you, Chaoqun," Chunting said as we walked along the dirt road. "I had an abortion."

"Really" was all I could say, my heart beating fast as I took in what she said.

She had become pregnant accidentally, and after the procedure had taken twenty days off to recover. "Little Song exhausts me. And do you know how expensive it is to raise a kid? I really can't understand why our parents cried over having a second child."

After Reform and Opening Up, Chinese people, especially my generation, were growing more open-minded. To my married friends, the need to carry on the family line was no longer their main concern. What mattered most was the financial burden of raising children. For years, China's fertility rate had been below replacement level. Experts were now saying that China faced a demographic crisis. In October 2015, the government encouraged all Chinese families to have a second child and demographers soon began discussing whether China should end birth limits entirely.

I found it ironic that so many babies had been killed during the One-Child Policy, and now those of us lucky enough to have survived, like me and Chunting, were being called on to produce more babies in the name of saving our country from a crisis. I could never forget the fact that I was not a "legal" baby and the sacrifices my parents had made to bring me into the world.

That evening, Chunting, Ling, and I had dinner together. Like other newly built homes in the village, the outer walls had been finished with trendy white tiles. As soon as one family in the village had done this, the rest quickly followed, some of them fearing the neighbors would think they could not afford renovations. Not to be outdone, Chunting and Ling had also installed new windows and doors. The floors were cool marble, and huge wedding photos took pride of place in the front rooms. Chunting never used her own kitchen so that it wouldn't get ruined, and would instead use her mother-in-law's.

Chunting said that almost all of the young people had moved to Lutai to live in apartments. The number of school-age children in the village had dwindled to the point that the local school was shut down, with Song sent to another village school, five miles away.

Much had changed, yet so much had also remained the same.

CHAPTER SIXTEEN

Forever Red

Uncle Lishui became an internet user at the age of seventy. Chunting bought him a smartphone, which changed his life. Initially, he had laughed and said he was too old to learn how to use it. But within a month, he had mastered it, and was sharing whatever he found interesting to our family chat group.

He had three favorite topics: reminiscing about the Mao era, North Korea, and current affairs. He didn't realize—at least initially—that so much of what was posted on the internet was total nonsense or nothing more than made-up rumors. His online friends were people who had similar interests, so social media kept him stuck in a time warp.

I changed jobs after three years at *That's Beijing* to work as a producer at Radio France International's Beijing Bureau; then, in the summer of 2016, I joined the *New York Times*'s Beijing bureau as a "researcher." Chinese law does not allow its citizens to be "journalists" employed by foreign-owned media; instead these writers are known officially as either "news assistant" or "researcher."

Still, I was excited about the job. I had been reading the *Times* ever since I was a university student—sometimes old copies in the library but more often their website with the help of a VPN. My teacher Helen had told me it's probably the most renowned paper in the world. The interview period lasted three months, and when I got the offer, I was traveling in Tibet with friends. We celebrated by drinking local bottles of beer—it was a dream coming true.

I was working on a piece about the Cultural Revolution, and thought Uncle Lishui would be the perfect person to interview. He had been a Red Guard. During the ten years of the Cultural Revolution, he had been offered two chances to work in the city, but he rejected them. He thought it was his duty to construct China's countryside, as Chairman Mao encouraged his youthful army to do. Uncle Lishui firmly believed that "in socialist China, there are no different classes." But after Reform and Opening Up, people chased after money and Mao's way went quickly out of date, with farmers like Uncle Lishui again looked down upon. Nobody really cared about making sacrifices for the country, and people laughed at Uncle Lishui's choice while he was young.

No matter how fiercely we argued about whether the Red Guards had damaged or tried to save the country, Uncle Lishui was forgiving. He loved me unconditionally, even if I disagreed with him. These days he was so proud of me that he bragged about me to his friends.

One autumn weekend, I visited Uncle Lishui just before the local elections.

Village committee members and village leaders began to be elected directly from 1998 onward, and are the only regularly held direct elections in China. These are attractive positions to hold; the officials not only manage the village's money but also have a chance to work with those in higher-level government. The village election is as close to democracy as Chinese people get, yet the system is riddled by bribery and cheating.

Each village committee has a chief, a party secretary, an accountant, and a person like Sister Lin in charge of work related to women. The village cadres manage collective enterprises, including land, building and repairing roads, maintaining public security, and administering family-planning issues. For a long time, that was all I knew about the village election apart from the fact that the previous village chief was a gangster. He'd wielded a knife and threatened to kill an entire family over a land dispute. Nobody dared to upset him in the election. The current chief, Lianrun, was not a gangster, but was just as greedy. When he learned that the central government was about to fund the restoration of riverbanks, he sectioned off a portion of the land by the river's edge and hastily built a shoddy six-room house. It was not for him to live in permanently. He knew that part of the budget had been reserved to compensate villagers whose homes would have to be demolished as part of the project. He received 100,000 yuan.

Lianrun announced that he was eager to run a second time. For the first time since he had been elected three years before, people could find him in his office, the potholes were fixed, and he let his office be used for public events. He knocked on doors and gave each family red en-velopes with money, and treated dozens of influential men in the village to a dinner at the fanciest restaurant in town.

Unsurprisingly, Lianrun was reelected.

"See, that's elections!" Uncle Lishui said to me. "He breaks promises and then he promises again. They're all corrupt. I don't see the difference between one wolf and another."

"It's not the fault of the election," I said. "It's the fault of certain people running."

Uncle Lishui believed that instead of elections China should have a leader as capable and strong-minded as Chairman Mao and that the central government should send somebody competent and with high moral standards to work as village officials. When Donald Trump won the presidential election in 2016, Uncle Lishui sent me an arti-cle that explained why Trump's winning set an example for China and the world that democracy was wrong. "Read this article. Are you still a fan of so-called American democracy? A businessman who is rude and arrogant is their president. Even I, a farmer, know he's nothing but a joke!"

★　　★　　★

In the autumn of 2017, China held the Nineteenth National Congress of the Communist Party. To mark the opening, the central government sent an environmental inspection team to our hometown and gave us a phone number so that we could report any violations of the environmental pro-tection rules. Uncle Lishui, who wanted to report on the garbage heaped near his house, dared not dial the number. Besides, everybody knew the biggest offender was the paper factory five miles away, which spilled its wastewater underground. The factory never got into trouble during environmental inspections.

Uncle Lishui called and asked if I could help him report the garbage. I encouraged him to make the call himself. "But," he said, "what if they tell the village officials that it was me?" My experiences were so unlike his. I never hesitated to say bad things. I angrily and openly criticized. I told him that his generation had been brainwashed into following suit and that nothing would happen to him.

I immediately regretted how cruel I sounded. Who was I to tell my uncle what he should and shouldn't believe in? He was an old man and had never been as privileged as I was lucky enough to be. My generation had abandoned him. He had made a way for us, but we criticized him and everything his generation had built.

So I dialed the number. After a dozen times with no answer, finally a stern-sounding woman said she would hand the information over to her boss. Nobody ever showed up.

CHAPTER SEVENTEEN

A People Without Roots

I had lost my hometown the moment I hopped on the bus and headed to university, and with each visit back, I struggled more than the previous time. I found it hard not to judge or look down on people. I wanted to stop them from being uncivilized—spitting, speaking loudly on the bus, and smoking indoors. I had lived in Beijing and thought I was somehow better. I had lost some ability to understand the local dialect I'd been speaking since childhood. I couldn't decipher their gestures, facial expressions, and subtle tones. Somewhere along the way, we had become different. They could also tell I was no longer the same. The restaurant owners would ask me what I was doing in their small place. The taxi drivers always charged me more money.

The only link between my hometown and me became the weekly phone call to my parents and my irregular weekend visits.

Almost as soon as I arrived, I couldn't wait to leave. I felt guilty, and promised to visit longer the next time, but always shortened my trip.

My childhood friends were all married. They'd half joke, "Bring your boyfriend next time or never show up again, Chaoqun." I felt ashamed but held my head high as they talked again about the same childhood memories, while I had been away experiencing new things. They seemed happy, working as policemen, low-level government clerks, or teachers, and posted photos of their children on social media, made the same jokes our parents did about their controlling husbands or wives.

I grew more at odds with my family—beyond bickering with Chunting about feminism. I couldn't help but want to change them. My mom thought the washing machine wasted too much water, so when she used it, she saved the water to rinse a basin or clean the toilet.

"It's getting smelly," I shouted one day, pouring the water into the sewer without her approval.

"It does not stink!" she demanded, racing over to grab the basin. "I prefer to wash my clothes by hand. All these new inventions are a waste of money."

"It's for your convenience, Mom." I kept pouring the water out.

"Wasting water is wasting money!"

"How much money would you save by re-using this water?"

"A few yuan today and a few yuan tomorrow make a lot. How do you think your father and I managed to send you and your brother to school? By always giving you whatever you wanted?"

They thought Yunxiang had changed too. A few years before, Yunxiang had married a woman from Lanzhou, a city in the northwest. Now they lived in Beijing and had a son. Yunxiang visited home even less than I did, partly because his city wife thought Lutai was a backwater. My mom went to Beijing a few times when my nephew was younger and needed somebody to look after him. But most of the time, it was Yunxiang's mother-in-law who helped. My mom didn't like Beijing, and felt conflicted.

Yunxiang bickered with my parents about similar things, too, those that seemed so country to us now. Our relatives in other villages always invited us to weddings, funerals, or their babies' one-month-old celebrations, but otherwise never. At those events, my parents were expected to give money or gifts. Needless to say, my parents always attended and even tried to take both Yunxiang and me along, arguing that it was the only opportunity we had to maintain relationships with our family. Yunxiang said there was no point in keeping up such relationships when he lived in Beijing and barely had enough time to be with the four of us.

"We can cut them off; what's the point of it?" he said one day when Baba insisted we go to the funeral of our grandfather's cousin.

"Does this mean you won't bring your son to my tomb when I die?" Baba asked in frustration. "No matter how far away you two go, your roots are still in the village!"

Yunxiang and I didn't reply. My parents couldn't even remember these people's names, so why did they feel obligated to pay their portion of a few hundred yuan at these ceremonies? Chinese people have many distant cousins and are expected to send money on such occasions. It had become a burden for us. My parents complained that we were unrealistic.

"They would talk badly about us if we didn't go and give money," said my father.

"Why do we have to live up to their expectations?" I countered.

"This is Lutai, not Beijing, remember that. What people say is all we have. You won't use your new city ways to embarrass our family," Mom scolded.

In Beijing, I was nostalgic about my hometown, which looked beautiful from afar. But though I felt I no longer belonged there, I knew I didn't belong to Beijing either.

Where do I belong? I'd wonder.

*   *   *

In the summer of 2015, I moved from the room I'd been renting for two years to the top floor in a *hutong* located in an older, characterful part of the city, closer to my office. My British friend, Oscar, was also looking for a new place, and asked me if I wanted to share a *hutong* house together. My salary had doubled, so I could finally move into a neighborhood that, in my mind, represented the spirit of Beijing.

Our house was complete with a yard and a rooftop terrace, and from my window I could watch the trees change with the seasons. On summer evenings, I liked to sit on the terrace, taking in the clouds transforming from red to purple as the sun set and flocks of pigeons flew through the sky. During the night, rain often dropped from leaves into a jar my neighbors kept under their window. *Plunk, plop.* In winter, I could reach out and feel the snowflakes. At my front door, I was greeted by the neighborhood ginger cat who would run toward me on top of the garden wall separating our house from the abandoned one next door. My "new" house was old, and full of stories. Though I had little money to spare and was unmarried, there wasn't anything nicer than sitting with a cup of hot tea and a book in the home I had created for myself. There, I began to love my life.

Baba said I was ridiculous: He didn't understand why in the world I wanted to live this way.

I had not told my parents that I was living with a guy— even though Oscar and I were just friends—and when Mom saw his clothes on the sofa while she video-chatted with me, she jumped to conclusions.

"No," I said. "It's not what you think. He has a girlfriend—and it's not me!"

"You're getting too wild. What are you doing? An unmarried woman living with a man? A *laowai*?" Mom's voice was shaking with anger, but, secretly, I had known they wouldn't be happy, and had done it to prove they should not care, or that I shouldn't. It was a small act of rebellion.

Our house in the *hutong* had clay-tiled floors, two good-size bedrooms, a small study, a spacious living room, a kitchen, and a bathroom, plus, of course, the roof terrace, where we sometimes held parties. We put up old film posters, threw down rugs over the cold tiles, and decorated the rooms with plants and a variety of lamps for atmosphere. The first floor had space enough to accommodate two couples and a divorcee. I didn't see her that often since she was dating someone, but I could hear one of the couples, who was always fighting.

The other couple, the Fengs, lived in the remaining two rooms. They were from Henan, and I liked them a lot. I would see them every day at around seven o'clock when I had finished work, and when they were usually cooking in their open-air kitchen.

They sold savory crepes filled with things like fried eggs, or chicken or vegetables, near the National Stadium or the "Bird's Nest," which had been one of the showcase venues of the 2008 Olympics and was now visited by many tourists. Located in the midst of a busy commercial center, the area teemed with white-collar workers.

Like most other breakfast vendors, they had converted their tricycle into a mobile, cooking-gas-fueled kitchen, small but perfectly formed and topped by a glass case to display the food. It was a humble job, but, one pancake after another, they had been able to send their two children to college. Their twenty-six-year-old daughter had graduated from one of the top universities in Beijing and now worked at a logistics company. Their son was studying at another university in Beijing and sometimes visited on the weekends.

Mr. Feng was friendly. Every day I saw him washing lettuce, chopping up chicken, or frying eggs to prepare for work the next morning. He always greeted me with: "You've come back?"

Mr. Feng's relatives lived next door and liked to grow pumpkins and cucumbers in small pots on their roof. As the vines grew, they trailed all the way to my door. The only way to get to their roof was by using the stairs in my yard, so I often met the woman holding a bucket of water at my door. Then we'd smile at each other and chat.

I liked the diversity of the people in the lively, mazelike *hutongs,* as well as the sense of community created there and which I hadn't felt since leaving Lutai. Young people would play music in a small guitar shop; a stray dog we called "Little Yellow" would wait for his friend Old Li, the dumpling-restaurant owner, to feed him; foreigners liked to sit around drinking Tsingtao beer, chatting, eating, at an outdoor barbecue place. At the fruit stand, the owner's daughter would sit outside doing her homework at a makeshift plywood desk. The recycling man, who used his electric tricycle to collect bags bursting full of crushed plastic bottles and collapsed, tightly tied cardboard boxes, would weave his way down the alleys and wave with a smile as he passed. We were all from different backgrounds, rich and poor, old and young, local and migrant, but we lived together harmoniously.

On weekends, if I stayed home, I would chat for hours with my neighbors. Many complained about the high cost of rent, and we'd laugh about the willy-nilly sense of the city we received in return. Urban planning had meant that so many beautiful ancient wooden structures like the *hutong* houses had been torn down, replaced by matchbox-like offices and glass-fronted hotels and apartment blocks.

The Fengs were considering moving back to Henan, their hometown. In the fifteen years they had lived in Beijing, they had saved enough money not only for their children's education but also for an apartment near their families. They joked that it was their dream to "dress in fine silk and return home like royalty." But their daughter did not want that. She had grown up in Beijing and knew nothing about Henan. She would not go with her parents if they chose to leave, nor would her brother.

The one thing that had encouraged the Fengs and other migrant workers to persevere was the belief that they would eventually "go home," and they were thrifty as possible in order to save. When they talked about Beijing, they spoke as if they were visiting. New things that happened in the city seemed to have nothing to do with them. But after ten years, fifteen years, twenty years, many of them remained.

What they didn't realize—or want to believe—was that their hometowns were also changing, the way people talked and dressed, and their habits. We had all become people without roots.

*   *   *

I was happy not only because of my new home but also because I had a new relationship. Two of my author friends and I had been speaking on a panel about Chinese youth, and Christian was in the audience. I had noticed him sitting in the second row, nodding when he agreed with what I said, which I appreciated since the panel was in English. When I got stuck on certain words and stammered, he would smile at me with encouragement.

He had a handsome face, reddish-blond hair, and deep,

melancholic eyes that seemed to belie a boyish curiosity. He looked thoughtful as he sat there and listened to us.

After the panel, Christian and I spent the evening talking only to each other, as if no one else existed. He was two years younger than I was, and had recently gotten a job at the *Financial Times*'s Beijing bureau as a junior reporter. We left the event together and bicycled in the same direction. It turned out we lived close by each other, and so it was even easier for us to start dating.

When my parents heard about my new relationship, the first thing my mom said was: "Bring him home."

CHAPTER EIGHTEEN

Coming Home

My neighbors Mr. and Mrs. Feng ignored their daughter's opposition and bought an apartment in Henan. If everything went well, they would leave Beijing within a year. Their son would graduate soon and they believed their city sojourn was reaching its end. One thing that pushed them to make the decision was the increasingly unfriendly attitude toward migrant workers.

Beijing had launched a "city beautification campaign," aiming to clear away tens of millions of illegal structures in the alleys, many of which were accommodations for *nongminggong*, "farmers-turned-workers" or low-income migrant workers, as well as the shops and restaurants where they worked and which catered to them.

The campaign was marketed as a way to improve the city aesthetically, as some renovations would also need to be done; however, it was no secret that the campaign was also an effort to "tackle urban diseases," as the media had dubbed them: overpopulation, increased traffic congestion, limited water resources, and pollution. The solution was simple and crude: push people out to the suburbs and other nearby regions. As the project quickly got under way, the sound of drills and jackhammers and revving dump trucks became almost constant. Without jobs or affordable housing, many low-income migrant workers found they had nowhere to work and could no longer afford to live in Beijing. They had to leave.

One day a demolition crew arrived in our *hutong* with forklifts and power saws, ready to take down a row of shops and houses. The owner of the beauty salon, who had replaced a brick-and-cement wall facing the street with a window to attract customers, was told the window ruined the look of the building. It had to be taken out, the wall restored, and the front door painted red. In fact, almost all doors in the *hutong* had to be repainted, as the government wanted to mimic and re-create an idealized version of Old Beijing.

The crew also removed red lanterns hanging in front of a Sichuan noodle restaurant, claiming these added too much personal design and were in danger of causing fires. They sealed the doors of many other shops and restaurants operating without a license, and demolished all the lean-tos and second floors that had been expanding for years haphazardly, house-of-cards-like.

They walked from alley to alley, sometimes themselves filling in unapproved windows and doors with cement blocks and bricks. My street looked as if it had been hit by an earthquake.

I was sad and angry to see people like the Fengs being pushed out. I wasn't a target, but what about next time?

What disappointed me most was that many local residents supported the campaign. They believed *nongminggong* made their city dirtier and noisier. Their reactions reminded me of how we had been treated when we first moved to Lutai. In reality, migrants didn't take anything from the locals. They had no health insurance, enjoyed no government aid, and did the jobs others turned their noses up at. They weren't parasites; quite the contrary, they contributed to our way of life in Beijing.

One day, when I returned from work, I saw Mr. Feng repairing his tricycle, both of his hands covered with so much black machine oil it looked as if he were wearing gloves.

"Finished with work?" he greeted me.

"Yes." I smiled. "Are you done early today? How's business?"

"Let's not talk about it. We're barely getting by," Feng said as he picked up a screwdriver to use on a handlebar. "Beijing isn't working for us anymore," Feng said, putting the screwdriver aside to sit on the steps and light a cigarette.

Street selling was, technically, illegal. But Beijing had tens of thousands of food peddlers skilled at dodging the authorities, who often just turned a blind eye. Now and then, *Chengguan*, the City Urban Administrative and Law Enforcement Bureau, would launch a raid. If they caught peddlers, they would take away their tricycles, which could be returned for a fine.

But Mr. Feng and his friends had made private "arrangements" with some of those working for the *Chengguan* so that they would be informed in advance of any raid.

This arrangement cost the peddlers a few yuan a day—
far less than any fine—and had worked for years. But recently, with Beijing's determination to push migrants out,
the *Chengguan* had ceased their protection racket. And the
inspections increased. Two-thirds of the food peddlers who
worked near the Bird's Nest stadium had already left.

That morning, the *Chengguan* almost caught Mr. Feng.
They arrived just as one of his customers was handing over
money for a crepe. When somebody shouted, "Run!" Feng
threw a handful of coins back to the customer, jumped on
his tricycle, and pedaled away fast as he could. When he
was making a turn, the tricycle toppled over, breaking the
handlebar and chain and the glass display case. By the time
I saw him, Feng had spent more than an hour trying to fix
it. The tricycle was all Feng had to make a living. I was worried about him, but didn't know how I could help.

Feng stood up, washed his hands in a bucket filled with
soapy water, and gestured toward the garage at the end of
the road. "I'll go to the mechanic," he said, and then it
dawned on us.

"Damn it, they even shut down the repair shop. Shit."

While I worried about Feng, I discovered that I might
also be affected. By the end of July, most second-floor apartments near the main streets had been demolished. If they
kept going, ours would also be knocked down, and I might
return one day, as one of my friends had, to find my landlord waiting to tell me I must move within three days
because my apartment was being demolished.

Beijing was like a spoiled child. The whole country fed
her its best resources. When she asked for something, she

got it. She could call people to her, work them to her ben-
efit, and when she didn't need them anymore, she would
kick them out anytime, without remorse.

★　★　★

Sure enough, I was affected but not yet in Beijing. Our *hu-*
tong in Lutai was going to be demolished. My neighbor
Wang Jianli's dream was finally coming true twenty years
after he had first talked about it.

Because some people were still dependent on dangerous
and polluting coal-fueled stoves to keep warm, the government planned to move them into apartments with central-
ized heating. Tianjin's newly appointed mayor, Xia Xin,
declared that there shouldn't be a "slum" in the center of
town, and that it would be removed. Tianjin was supposed
to be one of the most developed cities in the country, and Lutai was its suburb. It was not a slum, at least not to me. Every
family had their own yard and single-story home. "Well, the
mayor said it's a slum, so it's a slum," said my mom.

All residential buildings were destroyed if they were not
contemporary or high-rises. An announcement was posted
at the street-committee building:

> Great news! Dongdaying community will be demol-
> ished under the policy of the People-Benefiting Project.
> The plan is for each home to become an apartment, and
> the government will compensate your loss on indoor
> renovation and decoration. From now on, no family is
> allowed to make new construction or renovations to

their houses and should wait for the demolition team to
do the evaluation for compensation.

The offer was this: The government would take away all
the houses, replace them with new twenty-floor apartment
buildings on the site, and give the homeowners a modern home the same size as their old one. If anyone wanted
something bigger, they could purchase the extra space at
half the market price. Some found it reasonable, yet others
found it unacceptable. My parents were not happy with the
situation, but didn't want to fight with the government. So
they signed the agreement.

Suddenly the town was divided into two tribes. The pro-
leave people stopped talking to the pro-stay people. In
an odd juxtaposition, the former called the latter greedy,
thinking they were staying just to negotiate for more government benefits. Siblings fought with each other, and
children stopped talking to parents over inheritance issues. A woman showed up at my mom's school with a
bandage on her arm. Her brother had stabbed her with a
knife when she was negotiating with their parents for her
share of the compensation money.

And then there was Ms. Sun, a childless old woman who
would be particularly out of luck if she were rehoused. Ms.
Sun was nicknamed "Black Widow" because of her dark skin
and the fact that her husband had died twenty years earlier.
Nobody knew her first name. She ran a little farm shop that
she didn't have a permit for, and she never paid taxes. In
the late 1990s, after her husband died, she sold their one-
room house for 17,000 yuan and used some of the money to

build the little shop where she then worked and lived. Without planning permission for its construction, she wouldn't get anything from the government if it were demolished.

One day in September, another poster on the wall of the street-committee building announced: "Don't let the *dingzihu* get one penny more than the rest who sign the agreement earlier."

Dingzihu, or "nail households," meant families who disagreed with the demolition policy and compensation and refused to leave their house without a better offer. In recent years, the local government had started to care more about public opinion, thanks partly to the internet. Sometimes the *dingzihu* "won" and could remain living in their homes, though sometimes the government would then permanently cut off their access to power and water.

Many young people had moved away from Dongdaying when they married, so the *hutongs* were now filled mainly with older residents, who had lots of questions.

"I checked, and our apartment is only five hundred square feet. When you measured the house, you didn't count the kitchen and bathroom we built?" asked a neighbor, Zhao, during a community meeting with officials.

"No" was all one official said. His hair was unnaturally black against his very fair skin, and he sat with five other officials answering questions. Two young men sat at a desk and helped the homeowners sign their names on the agreement letter and information registration.

"But this is such a small apartment."

"You can buy extra space."

The neighborhood was forty years old. Nowhere in Lutai

was older. Living in an old neighborhood was a sign of being poor and backward, especially in small towns and cities, unlike in Beijing, where it had become fashionable. Chinese people usually despised old things, which they felt easier (and better) to replace than to repair.

★   ★   ★

Partly to appease my mom, I invited Christian to spend the Spring Festival with my family. I had never taken any guy back to Lutai, but I thought it would be polite to ask him, and that he might enjoy it. However, before he accepted, I had to warn him—to take a boyfriend home for this particular festival was as close as you could come to announcing your engagement. Weeks before our visit, I started to give "training" lessons to both Christian and my parents, who had never met a foreigner.

I warned my parents: "Don't ask about his salary or his parents' savings account balance. Don't stare at him as if he's an animal in the zoo. If you want to look at him carefully, I'll send you his photo. If he says he had enough food, don't push him to eat more."

And I told Yunxiang specifically, "Don't push Christian to drink too much *baijiu*. When he says he doesn't want any more, he means it."

"What should I say to people when they ask if you are getting married?" my mom asked.

"Oh, please. Come on, Mom!"

I warned Christian: "Please be prepared; they'll ask you awkward questions."

"Okay, no worries."

"And I hope you don't mind that they'll ask when you plan to buy an apartment for us, the wedding date, and other crazy things."

Christian was prepared. My family was prepared. But I was nervous.

*   *   *

Christian and I took the 7 a.m. bus to Ninghe, the name for the larger region of my hometown, including the areas of Chaoyang and Caiyuan villages and Lutai town. The bus was full, and before we boarded some passengers sat perched on their luggage or on the station floor.

I had told Christian a lot about where I had come from and how I had grown up, about the beautiful villages, the harvest in the autumn, the old people gossiping under trees, the many street dogs napping in the sun, the persimmons hanging on the trees like orange lanterns, and about my mom's cooking, which was the best in the world. When we drove out of Beijing, and along the deserted land, I began to see the journey and the countryside through Christian's eyes. The version I had described looked different from what we were passing along the way. I noticed tall, rusty-looking buildings, swampy, polluted-looking rivers, and plastic bags swirling around over farmland. I closed my eyes with embarrassment.

"We're here!" I woke Christian when we arrived at Lutai bus station.

He rubbed the sleep out of his eyes, shrugged on his backpack, and grabbed the bottle of *baijiu* he had bought as a gift.

"This is where I was born," I said as we made our way off the bus. "I hope you're not too disappointed."

"Of course not," he said, looking around. I knew he must be shocked by how different it was to the station in Beijing, where there were vending machines and benches. By comparison, Lutai station seemed really just a pile of gravel and broken bricks.

We took a taxi to my parents' house, where my brother, his wife, and my little nephew were waiting for us at the dinner table. I introduced Christian and we immediately sat down to eat. I was so nervous I could not look my parents in the eyes. I could tell they were on their best behavior, afraid to make mistakes in front of the young white man—oh, gosh, I wanted to run out of the room!

"Eat, eat" was all Mom said, over and over again. Because Christian was a vegetarian, she felt he must be hungrier than the rest of us. "Do you eat fish?" She moved the plate of braised silver carp closer to him and then picked it up to spoon some out for him.

"Sorry, I don't eat anything that has a face," Christian said shyly.

Mom stopped in midair, the plate still in her hand, and gently set it back down.

"Eating vegetables is good," Baba interjected, trying to defuse the awkward moment. "We don't know what the pigs are fed today."

I wanted to explain that Christian was an advocate for animal rights, but I knew nobody would be interested in that, or possibly even understand.

"Let's drink," Baba said, opening bottles of beer instead of the *baiju.*

Christian looked at me in defeat. I feigned a smile. I felt sorry for him. He looked totally overwhelmed.

When it was time for bed, my parents pulled me to the side to explain the sleeping arrangements. Yunxiang and Christian would sleep in one bedroom, my sister-in-law and I in another.

"Of course not," I chuckled. "Christian and I can sleep together, and Yunxiang and his wife can sleep together."

"What if other people hear about it?" Baba asked. "You're not married."

"Don't worry, nothing will happen. I will keep a distance from him, and no one will hear. But, please, it's strange if Yunxiang and Christian sleep in the same bed."

My parents looked at each other.

"And Yunxiang snores," I added. "Christian won't sleep well."

I had found a good excuse, and Mom made up the bed with two big quilts separated for each of us like sleeping bags.

"Wow, she really figured out how to keep us apart," Christian said when she left. We laughed, and I threw them together and locked the door.

The three days at home were full of dinners to celebrate the Spring Festival, which also marked the beginning of the Chinese new year. At one point, forty or so family members gathered in a restaurant set up with different tables—not one long one.

All the young couples had to approach the table of the elders and propose a toast for the New Year. One of my cousins, Hui, and her fiancé, Lai, went first.

"When are you getting married?" Aunt Zhirong asked them.

"This year, in August," she announced cheerfully.

"Great, great," everyone cheered, raising their glasses again. "That's good to hear."

Next was my turn. Hui and her boyfriend had been dating pretty much as long as Christian and I had, but I wasn't sure if I should do it myself or with Christian. I thought about running away, and pretending I'd forgotten, but my parents would have killed me. I waited for everybody else to finish, stood up, and turned to Christian. "Just follow me." He was confused and looked like a deer caught in the headlights, his face turning beet red.

"Happy New Year!" I said, without checking to see if Christian had arrived by my side.

My parents looked glad but nervous. They liked Christian, but my relationship with *laowai* was now public. It would be a big deal if we broke up. If you marry a foreign man, it's glorious, but if you break up with one, it stains your reputation worse than ever.

But I wasn't afraid anymore. We were often met with unfriendly stares from Chinese people on the bus, in the streets, the supermarket, everywhere, and I stared back. I had the right to choose whomever I wanted to be with.

★   ★   ★

On the last day of our visit, we gathered at my grandparents' tombs. We brought offerings of fruit, liquor, and
dumplings. Like most other village people, our family grave
was a set of tombs arranged on private farmland. During
the Cultural Revolution, many tombs like ours were destroyed, so the oldest ancestors ours contained were the
ashes of my great-grandparents. Resting behind them were
the tombs of my grandfather and his brothers.

According to Chinese custom, the urns are buried underground and marked with a little hill of earth. My mother
sprinkled some new earth atop the tombs and we all
weeded and tidied the site. We were "sweeping the graves"
as a mark of respect. I set down the offerings of fruit and
dumplings, and then Uncle Shoukui sprinkled *baijiu* over
the tombs of our male family members. We knelt, kowtowed, and then each took turns burning paper money for
the deceased.

The sunshine felt soft on my skin, and I inhaled the
smell of the burning paper and the liquor. Uncle Shoukui
spoke over the tombs, "We hope you are happy in another
world," and told them how much we missed them.

Many things had stayed the same in the twenty years
since my parents had moved us from the village to the
town. Our neighbors still played chess under the poplar
near the village chief's office, and the things that mattered
most were still the simplest: a sound marriage and happy,
healthy children, good food, plenty of work, and being responsible for your parents.

But many things had changed.

In villages today, shops sell everything from clothes and

cakes to scooters and cell phones; the internet is now available in most every household; every ten minutes, there is a bus going to the center of town; the roads have been paved with asphalt, and many young people own their cars, whether they need them or not. These are all considered indicators of progress or a better life—the kind of life my great-grandparent's and grandparent's generations once dreamed of.

In these small places, you can see the real China—its beauty and ugliness, the weird and familiar, the joyful and sad, progressive and backward at the same time. I've learned to cherish every ounce of it.

I'd been to the graves only a few times since my grandparents' burials, too busy living in the new China as it develops itself so rapidly before my eyes. My life and my country had become like a never-ending express train. We work hard to keep up and never pause to rest, feeling that the moment we stop, we would lose sight of the unknown something in the future that we're aiming to catch.

Acknowledgments

In the spring of 2008, at nineteen years old, I took the most important test of my life: the college entrance exam. As I memorized word after word, phrase after phrase of an alien language—English—I was motivated by my dream to become an author and tell Chinese stories to the outside world. It seemed like a fantasy. I was just a schoolgirl from a tiny town, whose life was confined to homework, the classroom, and the ten-minute walk in between.

Ten years later, that dream has come true. There are so many people who helped me grow from that deskbound girl to a published author.

My thanks go first to my family and childhood neighbors, who generously shared stories of their pasts and provided me with a firsthand history of what they lived through. They not only helped me understand my country and my people, but also became the material for this book. They taught me that the wisdom printed in the books I love comes first from the wisdom of real people working in the real world. To my parents, who gave all they could to provide me the best possible life, your kindness, wisdom, diligence, and optimism have supported and inspired me through hesitation and doubts. You taught me to always dream of a better life and then to make it happen. Your love is my life's greatest treasure.

To my primary and high school teachers, Li Shixia, Wang Yuying, and Dong Huimin, who gave endless encouragement to my writing dream. Your praise of my essays were my proudest moments at school. To my English teachers in high school and at university, Feng Quanxia, Sherry Yoder, and Mike Martucci, you showed me that English was so much more than just a language for small talk with foreigners.

To Leslie Jones, who I worked with at *That's Beijing Magazine*; to Robert Foyle Hunwick and Steve George, who trusted me to write longer and longer pieces and taught me lessons about writing that I still now am only just coming to fully appreciate. To Heike Schmidt and Edward Wong, who hired me to work at Radio France International and then the *New York Times* and showed me the ropes of journalism, a profession I remain passionate about and proud of.

A big thanks to Alec Ash, who first encouraged me to write personal essays and this book. You were a huge help, from editing my first book proposal to introducing me to my wonderful agent and providing helpful comments on my first draft.

Alec Ash's *Wish Lantern* and Eric Fish's *China's Millennials* served as exemplars while I wrote my own book. Zhang Lijia sat down with me and offered great advice on how to make scenes and language vivid and beautiful. Discussions with Tim Clissold helped me see afresh just how fascinating Chinese culture and history can be. Ian Johnson, Evan Osnos, and Xinran shared sage guidance on writing about China.

A lot of friends helped me polish my work at various stages: Amy Hawkins, Katrina Michelle, Zeben Kopchak, Oscar Holland, Gabriel Crossley, Dominique Wong, and Meredith Yang. You are great friends and editors.

I feel hugely fortunate to have worked at the *New York Times'* Beijing Bureau with talented and hardworking colleagues who are careful and close observers of China. You have provided a great service for the world in writing insightful stories about China, and I have learned a lot from you about reporting, interviewing, pitching, researching, and telling stories. The *Times* editors in Hong Kong and New York have taught me with great patience how to dig deeper and build a better-constructed final piece.

I am, of course, grateful to Krishan Trotman and Mollie Weisenfeld, my editors at Hachette Books, for their insightful readings and comments. Krishan's questions helped me understand my ideas better and to learn how to present stories in a captivating way. Massive thanks to my agent, Kelly Falconer at Asia Literary Agency, for her close reading of every word in my book, for thought-provoking comments, and for guiding a clueless first-time author through the world of publishing.

Special thanks to Christian Shepherd, who is always my first reader. You answered many bizarre questions on the differences between our cultures and have been an (almost always) patient English teacher. Your love, tolerance, and support give me the confidence to be me.

Index